Writing f

Figures in a Landscape

Writing from Australia edited by Wendy Morgan
Writing from Canada edited by Jim Rice and Mike Hayhoe
Writing from India edited by Lakshmi Holmström and Mike Hayhoe
Writing from Ireland edited by Valerie Quinlivan
Writing from South Africa edited by Anthony Adams and Ken Durham

Figures in a Landscape

Writing from India

Lakshmi Holmström and Mike Hayhoe

CAMBRIDGE
UNIVERSITY PRESS

Published by the Press Syndicate of the University of Cambridge

The Pitt Building, Trumpington Street, Cambridge CB2 IRP

40 West 20th Street, New York, NY 10011-4211, USA

10 Stamford Road, Oakleigh, Melbourne 3166, Australia

First published 1994

Printed in Great Britain at the University Press, Cambridge

A catalogue record for this book is available from the British Library

Library of Congress cataloguing in publication data applied for

ISBN 0 521 423805 paperback

Cover illustration: Roderick Johnson, 'India Railways', Images of India Picture
Agency, London

Contents

Acknowledgements

Choosing the tales and pictures for this book has been an important quest for us and we are grateful to many people. In particular, we should like to thank Gopal Gandhi (Director of The Nehru Centre, London), Usha Aroor (Orient Longman, Madras) and Gita Krishnankutty, author and translator, for their help during our research and selection; Vaya Naidu (storyteller) and Abhijit Pal (photographer) for their advice on the book's illustrations; Valerie Quinlivan (United World College of the Adriatic) and Alysoun Fenn (Hinchingbrooke High School) for their advice as practising teachers about our choice of stories; and Mark Holmström and Jean Hayhoe for their patience and support throughout this enterprise.

Thanks are due to the following for permission to reproduce illustrations: p.2 Lakshmi Holmström; p.34 and p.66 Victoria and Albert Museum; p.40 AP by John Moore; p.46 Anandakuttan; p.52 *India Today Magazine*; p.58 *La Belle Aurore*; p.88 Richard Lannoy; p.94 Robert Harding Picture Library Ltd; p.102 British Film Institute.

Thanks are due to the following for permission to reproduce stories: p.1 'Birthday' by Vijay Chauhan, permission granted by Amrit Rai and the translator Harish Trivedi; p.9 'Games at Twilight' by Anita Desai reproduced by permission of Rogers, Coleridge & White Ltd; p.17 'Can you Hear Silence?' by Shashi Deshpande, taken from *Intrusion & Other Stories* by Shashi Deshpande, reprinted with the permission of the author and Penguin Books India Pvt Ltd; p.25 'Passage' by Geeta Dharmarajan © Geeta Dharmarajan; p.33 'The First Party' by Attia Hosain, permission granted by Virago Press Ltd; p.39 'The Homecoming' by Arun Joshi © Arun Joshi; p.45 'The Bell' by Gita Krishnankutty © Gita Krishnankutty; p.51 'The Assignment' by Saadat Hasan Manto, translated by Khalid Hasan from *Kingdom's End and Other Stories*, reproduced by permission of Verso Books Ltd; p.57 'A Trip to the City' by Moti Nandi, translated by Enakshi Chatterjee, reprinted by permission of Moti Nandi and Enakshi Chatterjee; p.65 'The Disciple, The Jacana's Tale, The Three Piglets' by Suniti Namjoshi © Suniti Namjoshi; p.71 'Engine Trouble' by R.K. Narayan used by permission of Sheil Land Associates Ltd; p.79 'The Homecoming' by Mrinal Pande © Mrinal Pande; p.87 'January Night' by Premchand, reproduced courtesy of the publishers

(Penguin Books India Pvt Ltd) and the translator; p.95 'Stench of Kerosene' by Amrita Pritam translated by Khushwant Singh, used by permission of Jaico Publishing House; p.101 'We Have Arrived in Amritsar' by Bhisham Sahni © Bhisham Sahni; p.113 'A Day with my Father' by Sundara Ramaswamay translated by Lakshmi Holmström © Sundara Ramaswamay and Lakshmi Holmström.

Every attempt has been made to locate copyright holders for all material in this book. The publishers would be glad to hear from anyone whose copyright has been unwittingly infringed.

Introduction

How can I convey to you the variety of landscapes and languages, customs and cultures that make up the country I know as India?

Let us say that I arrive in New Delhi, the capital of India, after an eight-hour flight from London. My journey will only have begun, for I will want to go on to Tamil Nadu in the south, the state where I was born and grew up. To get to its capital city, Madras, by train from New Delhi will take me about thirty-four hours: two nights and a day. I leave New Delhi, not only an elegant modern capital and the seat of the central government, but also the site of a succession of ancient cities, at 10.30 p.m.

The train starts on its journey south. During the night it passes Mathura, legendary city of the god Krishna; Agra, where the Taj Mahal stands; and then the fortified city of Gwalior. We go through a bustling railway junction at Jhansi, a town every Indian child knows for its Queen Lakshmibai, who made a brave stand against the British colonisers in the nineteenth century. The train travels through the huge state of Madhya Pradesh, crosses the Vindhya Mountains and arrives by late morning at Nagpur. We are now in another state, Maharashtra. The signboards are in Marathi, not in Hindi any more. Men and women wear clothes which are very different from those worn in the north. I must buy oranges in Nagpur – the place is famous for them. Southwards again over a huge bridge over the Godavari River, and by late afternoon we are crossing the Telugu-speaking state of Andhra.

Very early the next morning we are speeding along the south-eastern coast of India. The landscape begins to look more familiar to me: rice paddies edged with coconut palms, huge sculpted stone temple towers in the distance. At the first station I buy my south Indian breakfast of steamed *idlis*, served with a spicy lentil sauce. Before I know it, we have slipped into Tamil Nadu and at 7.50 a.m. we arrive in Madras.

India is many Indias, many people, many cultures and many languages; this book is a collection of stories from this complex and exciting country, some written in English and many translated from its wide variety of languages and ways of telling stories.

There are seventeen major languages in India, each with its own pronunciation and its own writing system. The map on page xiv gives you a rough idea of where these are used: for example, Panjabi in the northern state of Panjab; Bengali in West Bengal (and in the now separate nation called Bangladesh); Gujarati in the western state of Gujarat and Telugu in the eastern state of Andhra Pradesh. But that is far too simple. In some states, more than one major language is spoken and in several there are lots of minor, tribal languages, as in Bihar. And then there is the constant movement of people, for all sorts of reasons, across the length and breadth of the country. They take their native language with them and, if they settle, learn yet another. Finally, at different times, different languages have been 'privileged' – have had the most power and prestige. The ancient language of Sanskrit remains important as the language of the great Hindu literary classics and scriptures. Urdu comes from the time when Muslim nations from the North and West invaded and settled in India. Hindi, a modern descendant of Sanskrit, is now spoken by roughly a third of India's population, the biggest minority language. English was imported by the British when they invaded and colonised India, and it remains a much-used language among the educated.

What might surprise you is that most Indian children grow up hearing, and then speaking, more than one language. This is probably one of the most creative skills that they learn, for it means that they can think and feel and express themselves within more than one culture. A. K. Ramanujan explains how his 'father tongues' were used by his father – English to help him understand the imposed orderliness of colonial India, and English and Sanskrit to understand the stars – and how his mother used her 'mother tongues' to help him maintain living contact with the exciting 'ordinary' world which surrounded his home.

As we grew up, Sanskrit and English were our father tongues, and Tamil and Kannada were our mother tongues. The father tongues distanced us from our mothers, from our own childhoods, and from the villages and many of our neighbours in the cowherd colony next door. And the mother tongues united us with them. It now seems quite appropriate that our house had three levels: a downstairs for the Tamil world, an upstairs for the English and the Sanskrit, and a terrace on top that was open to the sky where our father could show us the stars and tell us their English and Sanskrit names. From up there on the terrace, we could also look down on the cowherd colony, and run noisily and breathlessly for a closer look if we saw the beginnings of a festival, a wedding, or a 'hair to hair' fight between two women (with the choicest obscenities pouring from them), or a magnificent *vilayti*, or foreign bull, brought specially to service the local cows.

We ran up and down all these levels. Sanskrit, English, and Tamil and Kannada . . . stood for three different, interconnected worlds.

A. K. Ramanujan, 'Telling tales', *Daedalus*, Fall 1989, p. 241

I think that 'interconnected' is the key word in this description.

The use of the English language in India has a special history. In 1589, the British first arrived as traders in 'India' (the Indian subcontinent), although it was not until 1848, after more than two centuries of trade and colonisation, that India was declared part of the British Empire. English became widely used as an official language and in universities from the 1840s onwards. Today, it remains in many ways the language of the middle classes across the country. This gives it both advantages and limitations.

You will see, for example, that some of the stories written in English in this collection describe the lives of middle-class people in unnamed modern cities; look at Attia Hosain's 'The First Party', Arun Joshi's 'The Homecoming' and Anita Desai's 'Games at Twilight'.

But not all the stories written in English suggest a background that is nameless and which could be anywhere in modern, urban India. Geeta Dharmarajan's 'Passage', R. K. Narayan's 'Engine Trouble' and Gita Krishnankutty's 'The Bell' all happen in places where you feel that the characters belong. In these stories, you can see how over the years English has become another of India's languages, picking up and describing local scenes, thoughts and feelings. Indeed, long familiarity with English has helped writers from throughout India to take liberties with it, to bend and change it and even re-invent it so that it has become their own language and not simply a reminder of when India was a colony.

We have chosen stories which span something like seventy years, to reflect in a small way the historical change that India has experienced in that time. Premchand's 'January Night', published in 1930, shows you how tenant farmers were exploited by absentee landlords who lived off the rents they extracted from such poor people. The peasantry were frequently driven off the land on which they depended for survival and were forced to seek work in towns. Here, as elsewhere in the world, the rural poor were forced to move from the countryside into the cities – the land emptied as the cities started to swell.

India's most important event this century took place in 1947 when the subcontinent was partitioned into two independent states, India and Pakistan. The process was fraught with distress and violence, and it continues to be a vivid and violent theme in many stories, such as those we have included by Manto and Bhisham Sahni. But India has continued to experience great political conflict since Independence. Arun Joshi's 'The Homecoming' captures the feelings of a soldier returning from the Bangladesh Liberation War of 1971 (another breaking away).

It is true that several of these stories describe change, uncertainty and even tragedy in India as a nation, but that is only one of the aspects that they seek to suggest to you. Earlier on, I spoke of the importance of the family, and how it often gives children two or more languages. It is striking how important families and family life are throughout this collection. There is a strong sense of family life, even when there is restlessness or change, as in Sundara Ramaswamy's 'A Day with My Father', or Mrinal Pande's 'The Homecoming', where the family property has been sold off amidst unhappy bickering, or Vijay Chauhan's 'Birthday', when the children have all gone their different ways.

The family, then, is central to many of these tales and to people's lives. You may notice that in these tales, families contain only children and adults. Few focus on the western idea of adolescence. Instead, people pass from childhood to adulthood seamlessly. For example, Giribala, the wise and compassionate wife in Moti Nandi's 'A Trip to the City', is only seventeen. The children in Chauhan's 'Birthday', are only a little younger than their older brother Bhai Saheb, who, as the oldest male in the family, has his duties to carry out as head of the household.

Perhaps it will surprise you that Indian writers do not focus on courtship or love in a western, 'romantic' sense. (The nearest equivalent to that is present, perhaps, in Amrita Pritam's 'Stench of Kerosene', which juxtaposes a first marriage which is based on romantic choice with a second which is brought about through convenience and obeying tradition.) Instead, several of these stories are built around the relationship between a husband and a wife who are married according to tradition, exploring it carefully and subtly in a variety of ways. The marriage in Ramaswamy's 'A Day with My Father' is almost certainly one that has been arranged according to custom. It is worth reading, to see how they communicate through all kinds of signals, which the children in the story are quick to pick up and decode.

The relationship between the tailor and his wife in Geeta Dharmarajan's 'Passage' is a troubled one and sits between the traditional and the new. Here again, it is worth seeing how their being together relies on a variety of signals and codes. Perhaps learning to read about another culture involves learning to read not only its verbal language or languages but also its other languages of gesture and ritual. For me, one of the valuable things about stories is that they help us to do precisely that.

I hope these stories will help you realise that there is no such thing as a changeless, timeless India. The picture that emerges from them for me is of a nation that is constantly undergoing change; of boundaries being staked out, only to be broken down; of confrontations and negotiations between old and new at many levels and in many ways. Perhaps that is why the theme of the journey – of going away and, sometimes, of coming back – is so powerful in this collection. Indeed, one of the most frequent images is that of the train from which the changing landscape is viewed. Tales and trains are my own favourite ways of 'seeing' my country, India.

Lakshmi Holmström

Note to readers: Unfamiliar words appear in italics the first time they are mentioned in each story. Explanations to these are provided in the glossary.

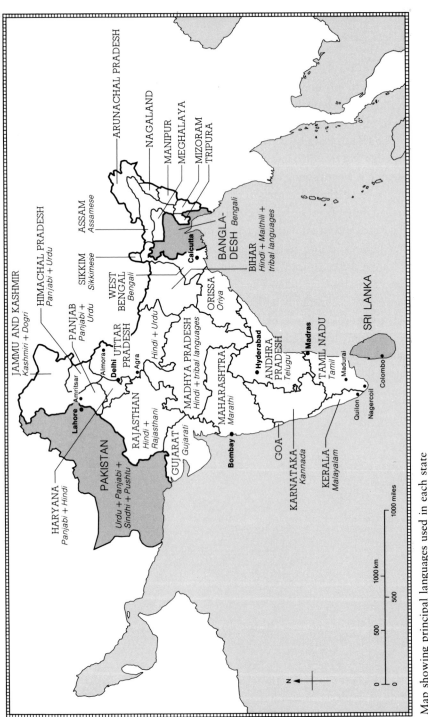

Map showing principal languages used in each state

Birthday

VIJAY CHAUHAN 1990

Translated from Hindi by H. K. Trivedi

This gentle story is set in a small town, probably in the northern state of Uttar Pradesh. Its narrator remembers with affection the quarrelsome rituals that used to take place when he was a boy, as various servants and tradespeople sought to retain his family as customers. The significant point is that the parents are dead and that his 'Bhai Saheb', the eldest brother, has had to take on the burden of being head of the family. At the end of the tale, so much has altered and, for the narrator, may be lost.

We used to keep up till late at night, and get up quite early in the morning. There was no need to get up so early, except that once we were awake there seemed no point in lolling about in bed. If we got up, we could have had a cup of tea.

There was, however, just a little snag to having tea, which was that our paraffin-stove was not easy to light. We would first stop the air vent and then pump, till the oil came gushing out. As soon as we put a match to it, the oil would burst out in flames. The wall behind was black with soot right up to the ceiling. When all the oil had burnt out, we would pump again, furiously, but this resulted in merely another thin spurt of oil. Opening the air vent, we would let the oil flood out again. After a few moments, we would light it again, and pump again. Only after this process had been repeated several times would our stove be finally lit. Having put some water on, we would then begin the long wait for the milkman. God knows how many times we had told him, but he never came on time. Each day, before accepting his milk, we would have the same argument. 'So, you have found time at last to come to us, after completing the whole round. If you are late again tomorrow, we'll settle your account then and there.'

The milkman would say, 'Yes, *bhaiya*, I really am late today. Never been so late before, have I?'

'Yes, of course you have. In fact, have you ever been on time?'

Family photograph, 1906

The milkman would keep quiet.

'And less of water in the milk, do you hear?' our little sister would add.

Whenever we told him off for coming late, he would admit his fault at once. When he himself promised never to be late again nor to add any water to the milk, we had not the heart to go on.

It was the same with Gajji, our *dhobi*. Often, two Sundays would pass one after another without a glimpse of Gajji. Even if one had a lot of clothes – which we did not – one could not have had so many that one could simply keep pulling them out of the trunk and, having worn them, casting them off into the wicker-basket in the corner, without coming to an end of them. Some days before the second Sunday, we would begin fretting about what we were going to wear next. From among the shirts piled up on the pegs, we would begin selecting a 'clean' one. And when there weren't any more 'clean' clothes left, we would, on the Sunday morning, pace the veranda in a wrap-around, and just wait for Gajji to turn up.

When he came, he would park his bicycle some distance away in the courtyard, and untie the bundle of clothes from the carrier. We would already have thought up three or four days in advance, and rehearsed several times over, precisely what we would say to him. Bearing the bundle, his eyes downcast, he would now approach the veranda. He would put down the bundle on the floor, and begin untying it.

'Take these clothes away. We don't want them.'

He'd just sit there, his head bowed. Were he to answer, we could shout some more. When he'd still be quiet after some more time, denying us further opportunities, we would ask, 'What's the matter? Why don't you say something?'

Now he would speak, in a hushed tone, 'Death in the family.'

'Oh dear!' we'd exclaim.

The dhobi would continue, 'Aunt passed away. Had to arrange for the funeral. Nobody else to do it. Left small kids. Have brought them all home.'

Silently we would share in his grief.

'It's only your clothes I have brought today; the others' aren't even washed yet. This death held up things, or has Gajji ever been late before?'

By now he would have untied the bundle.

'Bring the notebook; come now, tick them off.' We'd run and get the notebook, and begin calling out the items.

God knows how many aunts and other assorted aged relatives our dhobi had, who were only too willing to oblige him by popping off whenever he was in fear of getting shouted at for being late. Thus it had been for countless years. We would not shout at him at the time, for fear that what he was telling us might be the truth, but we always felt later on that he had again got away with it. Whenever we asked him afterwards, he would laugh and say, 'What to do, bhaiya, I had to lie, for there were all of you, just waiting to blow your top off. Any other excuse, and I would have had it!'

Both the dhobi and the tailor had another mighty hold on us: 'We have been serving this house since the days of your *Babuji* and your mother.' Our dhobi, in fact, would even wipe tears from his eyes as he said this.

Whenever our tailor, Siddique Master visited us, we'd say, '*Masterji* is here! Let's have some tea for him.' Then, we would all sit together and have tea. *Paan* would be sent for, for he liked paan. Then alone could we begin to talk business. We'd all bring out our pieces of cloth, which we had bought with such care and enthusiasm.

'Look, Masterji, I must have my tweed jacket by the twenty-fifth.'

Someone else would say, 'And my suit, too, by the same date. You know, I want to wear it this winter, not the next.'

We would all submit our requirements to Masterji. He would take measurements, enter all the particulars in *Urdu* in his notebook, gather up the pieces of cloth, and, promising to have everything ready by the due date, depart.

We would start hanging around his shop from the twenty-second onwards. When we entered the shop, he would clear off a part of the ironing board and say, 'Take a seat, bhaiya.'

A boy would be sent off for tea and paan. Having drunk tea and chewed the paan, we would mention our clothes, and Masterji would say, 'Of course, they'll be ready by the twenty-fifth. Send somebody round for them at, say, about five.'

'But five would be too late! Can't we have them by three o'clock?'

'But the party is at six, isn't it? All right, everything will be ready at four.' We would return home. The twenty-fifth would arrive, it would be four o'clock, and we'd send Ram Singh to Masterji's shop, but the clothes would still be unfinished. We would be mad with anger. We would look reproachfully at *Bhai Saheb*, and he would say, 'What are you looking at me for? Did I ever ask you to go to that man?'

Nevertheless, no tailor was ever allowed to cross our threshold except Siddique Master.

We had Ram Singh to cook for us. He had come to us several years ago, from Ranikhet. Once or twice a month, he would get home-sick. This meant that he would tie a handkerchief tightly round his forehead, and go and lie down in his room. We never woke him up to get the morning tea for us; we thought he might not like to get up so early. On the days he would not emerge from his room at all, we knew he must be feeling home-sick. One of us would go to him to make the necessary enquiries. He would be lying there on his *charpoy*, covered with a sheet.

'So, what's up, Ram Singh? No plans to cook today?'

From underneath the sheet a voice would answer, 'Terrible headache.'

To prove the headache, the head would emerge from the sheet, a handkerchief wound tightly round it.

'You haven't a fever, have you?'

His pulse would be felt, some tablet or the other would be given to him for the pain, and then we would all sit in conference over his sickness.

'Excuses, excuses!'

'How do you know? Remember what you feel like when you have a headache?'

'We didn't shout at him yesterday, did any one?'

The discussion would then proceed along familiar channels. 'He's always like this when he feels home-sick.'

'If he's home-sick, why does he take to his bed like this, with that handkerchief?'

'He only feels home-sick when he's been ticked off.'

'But none of us said anything to him yesterday.'

Then we would all look at each other. We would review the events of the previous day, in order to find out what could possibly have offended him.

Communication would be established once again with Ram Singh. Another round of negotiations would begin.

'You are not feeling home-sick, are you?'

No reply.

Mention then would be made of the particular incident which was supposedly gnawing at his heart. Attempts would be made to explain that nobody had wanted to hurt him, for wasn't he, in fact, one of the family?

'We feel that you are simply one of us. Don't we quarrel among ourselves?

How often do we say things to each other, but none of us shuts himself up in a room to sulk, with a handkerchief tied round his forehead! If you prefer it, we can also begin treating you like a servant, as they do elsewhere. But you will not like that, nor shall we.'

Having listened to all this and having considered everything, he would untie the handkerchief and go to the kitchen and begin to cook.

Then, we would start on another debate. 'After all, why are we so devoted to this Ram Singh? Why don't we chuck him out? For how long can we continue to pamper him like this?'

'We shall never find another man half as good. Whatever else he may be, he is at least honest.'

'So, *he* can take offence, but *we* mustn't!'

We never did chuck Ram Singh out. When his home-sickness grew worse, we gave him the afternoon off on Sundays, and even promised to send him to Ranikhet for three months in a year.

We had great arguments over all these matters, but it wasn't as if we did not quarrel enough by ourselves.

Bhai Saheb was often late returning for lunch. Sometimes it would get to be two o'clock. All of us would wait for him, and when he eventually came, we used to explode. 'Nothing can be more important than lunch.'

'You care more for that lot than for your own folk!'

'It's just impossible for you ever to be on time.'

'We have grown limp with hunger, just sitting and waiting.'

'When one is out and busy, one doesn't feel so hungry. If you were to sit at home and wait, you'd soon find out!'

Bhai Saheb would sometimes keep quiet, and sometimes give as good as he got. We called him Bhai Saheb, but he wasn't older by all that much.

We would all eat in silence, but once the food was inside us, it used to be all right. Bhai Saheb would say, 'You will not believe it, but one thing just kept cropping up after another, and I was held up.'

There was but one bathroom in the house. Whenever any of us wanted to bathe, there were always quarrels, for none of us had a fixed hour for bathing. If anyone found the bathroom occupied, he'd say, 'Who is this always in there, whenever it's time for me to bathe?'

Then, he'd proceed to knock on the door. And then ask, 'Who is this inside?'

There would come the answer, 'Would it help if you knew? Whoever it is in here must be bathing, mustn't he?'

'Come out quickly!'

'How quickly?'

'At once!'

'Can't!'

In the dining room, there were never enough chairs for everybody. Three of us always had to pull chairs or stools out from other rooms. God knows why it never struck us to order three more chairs, and thus to put an end to the perpetual dispute regarding seating at meal-times. Whoever entered the dining room late had to provide a seat for himself. This applied even to guests.

'Why must you occupy *my* place everyday?'

'And how has it become *your* place?'

'Because it is!'

'I will not get a stool from the drawing room day after day. Whoever it is who sets the table must also arrange for seats for everybody.'

'Just go on sermonising like this for a bit longer, and even the food will be all gone.'

Such, such were the days. Today, on a birthday, a whole host of memories come to mind. Now, there are no such problems. There is a huge house with three bathrooms, enough clothes for one not to bother about when the dhobi will turn up, and there is even a punctual enough tailor. The brothers and sisters have all gone their own ways. My work keeps me occupied all day, but it still hurts when I remember that childhood, which has now been left far behind.

Games at Twilight

ANITA DESAI 1978

Anita Desai sets her tale in a large, modern city, but which one it might be is of no importance. It is all too easy to assume that being middle-class, prosperous and privileged guarantees happiness. But childhood can be a time of intense grief in any circumstances, including simply playing games. What begins as a game of hide-and-seek one hot afternoon turns to personal tragedy for the little boy, Ravi, as his dreams of triumph collapse into fear and rejection.

It was still too hot to play outdoors. They had had their tea, they had been washed and had their hair brushed, and after the long day of confinement in the house that was not cool but at least a protection from the sun, the children strained to get out. Their faces were red and bloated with the effort, but their mother would not open the door, everything was still curtained and shuttered in a way that stifled the children, made them feel that their lungs were stuffed with cotton wool and their noses with dust and if they didn't burst out into the light and see the sun and feel the air, they would choke.

'Please, Ma, please,' they begged. 'We'll play in the *veranda* and porch – we won't go a step out of the porch.'

'You will, I know you will, and then – '

'No – we won't, we won't,' they wailed so horrendously that she actually let down the bolt of the front door so that they burst out like seeds from a crackling, overripe pod into the veranda, with such wild, maniacal yells that she retreated to her bath and the shower of talcum powder and the fresh sari that were to help her face the summer evening.

They faced the afternoon. It was too hot. Too bright. The white walls of the veranda glared stridently in the sun. The *bougainvillaea* hung about it, purple and magenta, in livid balloons. The garden outside was like a tray made of beaten brass, flattened out on the red gravel and the stony soil in all shades of metal – aluminium, tin, copper and brass. No life stirred at this arid time of day – the birds still drooped, like dead fruit, in the papery tents of the trees; some squirrels lay limp on the wet earth under the garden tap. The outdoor dog lay stretched as if dead on the veranda mat, his paws and ears and tail all reaching out like dying travellers in search of water. He rolled his eyes at the children – two white marbles rolling in the purple sockets, begging for sympathy – and attempted to lift his tail in a wag but could not. It only twitched and lay still.

Then, perhaps roused by the shrieks of the children, a band of parrots suddenly fell out of the eucalyptus tree, tumbled frantically in the still, sizzling air, then sorted themselves out into battle formation and streaked away across the white sky.

The children, too, felt released. They too began tumbling, shoving, pushing against each other, frantic to start. Start what? Start their business. The business of the children's day which is – play.

'Let's play hide-and-seek.'

'Who'll be It?'

'You be It.'

'Why should I? You be – '

'You're the eldest – '

'That doesn't mean – '

The shoves became harder. Some kicked out. The motherly Mira intervened. She pulled the boys roughly apart. There was a tearing sound of cloth but it was lost in the heavy panting and angry grumbling and no one paid attention to the small sleeve hanging loosely off a shoulder.

'Make a circle, make a circle!' she shouted, firmly pulling and pushing till a kind of vague circle was formed. 'Now clap!' she roared and, clapping, they all chanted in melancholy unison: 'Dip, dip, dip – my blue ship . . .' and every now and then one or the other saw he was safe by the way his hands fell at the crucial moment – palm on palm, or back of hand on palm – and dropped out of the circle with a yell and a jump of relief and jubilation.

Raghu was It. He started to protest, to cry 'You cheated – Mira cheated – Anu cheated . . .' but it was too late, the others had all already streaked away. There was no one to hear when he called out, 'Only in the veranda – the porch – Ma said – Ma *said* to stay in the porch!' No one had stopped to listen, all he saw were their brown legs flashing through the dusty shrubs, scrambling up brick walls, leaping over compost heaps and hedges, and then the porch stood empty in the purple shade of the bougainvillaea and the garden was as empty as before; even the limp squirrels had whisked away, leaving everything gleaming, brassy and bare.

Only small Manu suddenly reappeared, as if he had dropped out of an invisible cloud or from a bird's claws, and stood for a moment in the centre of the yellow lawn, chewing his finger and near to tears as he heard Raghu shouting, with his head pressed against the veranda wall, 'Eighty-three, eighty-five, eighty-nine, ninety . . .' and then made off in a panic, half of him wanting to fly north, the other half counselling south. Raghu turned just in time to see the flash of his white shorts and the uncertain skittering of his red sandals, and charged after him with such a bloodcurdling yell that Manu stumbled over the hosepipe, fell into its rubber coils and lay there weeping, 'I won't be It – you have to find them all – all – All!'

'I know I have to, idiot,' Raghu said, superciliously kicking him with his toe. 'You're dead,' he said with satisfaction, licking the beads of perspiration off his upper lip, and then stalked off in search of worthier prey, whistling spiritedly so that the hiders should hear and tremble.

Ravi heard the whistling and picked his nose in a panic, trying to find comfort by burrowing the finger deep – deep into that soft tunnel. He felt himself too exposed, sitting on an upturned flower pot behind the garage. Where could he burrow? He could run around the garage if he heard Raghu come – around and around and around – but he hadn't much faith in his short legs when matched against Raghu's long, hefty, hairy footballer legs. Ravi had a frightening glimpse of them as Raghu combed the hedge of *crotons* and *hibiscus*, trampling delicate ferns underfoot as he did so. Ravi looked about him desperately, swallowing a small ball of snot in his fear.

The garage was locked with a great heavy lock to which the driver had the key in his room, hanging from a nail on the wall under his work-shirt. Ravi had peeped in and seen him still sprawling on his string-cot in his vest and striped underpants, the hair on his chest and the hair in his nose shaking with the vibrations of his phlegm-obstructed snores. Ravi had wished he were tall enough, big enough to reach the key on the nail, but it was impossible, beyond his reach for years to come. He had sidled away and sat dejectedly on the flower pot. That at least was cut to his own size.

But next to the garage was another shed with a big green door. Also locked. No one even knew who had the key to the lock. That shed wasn't opened more than once a year when Ma turned out all the old broken bits of furniture and rolls of matting and leaking buckets, and the white ant-hills were broken and swept away and *Flit* sprayed into the spider-webs and rat-holes so that the whole operation was like the looting of a poor, ruined and conquered city. The green leaves of the door sagged. They were nearly off their rusty hinges. The hinges were large and made a small gap between the door and the walls – only just large enough for rats, dogs and, possibly, Ravi to slip through.

Ravi had never cared to enter such a dark and depressing mortuary of defunct household goods seething with such unspeakable and alarming animal life but, as Raghu's whistling grew angrier and sharper and his crashing and storming in the hedge wilder, Ravi suddenly slipped off the flower pot and through the crack and was gone. He chuckled aloud with astonishment at his own temerity so that Raghu came out of the hedge, stood silent with his hands on his hips, listening, and finally shouted 'I heard you! I'm coming! *Got* you – ' and came charging round the garage only to find the upturned flower pot, the yellow dust, the crawling of white ants in a mud-hill against the closed shed door – nothing. Snarling, he bent to pick up a stick and went off, whacking it against the garage and shed walls as if to beat out his prey.

Ravi shook, then shivered with delight, with self-congratulation. Also with fear. It was dark, spooky in the shed. It had a muffled smell, as of graves. Ravi had once got locked into the linen cupboard and sat there weeping for half an hour before he was rescued. But at least that had been a familiar place, and even smelt pleasantly of starch, laundry and, reassuringly, of his mother. But the shed smelt of rats, ant-hills, dust and spider-webs. Also of less definable, less recognisable horrors. And it was dark. Except for the white-hot cracks along the door, there was no light. The roof was very low. Although Ravi was small, he felt as if he could reach up and touch it with his fingertips. But he didn't stretch. He hunched himself into a ball so as not to bump into anything, touch or feel anything. What might there not be to touch him and feel him as he stood there, trying to see in the dark? Something cold, or slimy – like a snake. Snakes! He leapt up as Raghu whacked the wall with his stick – then, quickly realising what it was, felt almost relieved to hear Raghu, hear his stick. It made him feel protected.

But Raghu soon moved away. There wasn't a sound once his footsteps had gone around the garage and disappeared. Ravi stood frozen inside the shed. Then he shivered all over. Something had tickled the back of his neck. It took him a while to pick up the courage to lift his hand and explore. It was an insect

– perhaps a spider – exploring *him*. He squashed it and wondered how many more creatures were watching him, waiting to reach out and touch him, the stranger.

There was nothing now. After standing in that position – his hand still on his neck, feeling the wet splodge of the squashed spider gradually dry – for minutes, hours, his legs began to tremble with the effort, the inaction. By now he could see enough in the dark to make out the large solid shapes of old wardrobes, broken buckets and bedsteads piled on top of each other around him. He recognised an old bathtub – patches of enamel glimmered at him and at last he lowered himself onto its edge.

He contemplated slipping out of the shed and into the fray. He wondered if it would not be better to be captured by Raghu and be returned to the milling crowd as long as he could be in the sun, the light, the free spaces of the garden and the familiarity of his brothers, sisters and cousins. It would be evening soon. Their games would become legitimate. The parents would sit out on the lawn on cane basket chairs and watch them as they tore around the garden or gathered in knots to share a loot of mulberries or black, teeth-splitting *jamun* from the garden trees. The gardener would fix the hosepipe to the water-tap and water would fall lavishly through the air to the ground, soaking the dry yellow grass and the red gravel and arousing the sweet, the intoxicating scent of water on dry earth – that loveliest scent in the world. Ravi sniffed for a whiff of it. He half-rose from the bathtub, then heard the despairing scream of one of the girls as Raghu bore down upon her. There was the sound of a crash, and of rolling about in the bushes, the shrubs, then screams and accusing sobs of 'I touched the den – ' 'You did not – ' 'I did – ' 'You liar, you did *not*' and then a fading away and silence again.

Ravi sat back on the harsh edge of the tub, deciding to hold out a bit longer. What fun if they were all found and caught – he alone left unconquered! He had never known that sensation. Nothing more wonderful had ever happened to him than being taken out by an uncle and bought a whole slab of chocolate all to himself, or being flung into the *soda-man's* pony cart and driven up to the gate by the friendly driver with the red beard and pointed ears. To defeat Raghu – that hirsute, hoarse-voiced football champion – and to be the winner in a circle of older, bigger, luckier children – that would be thrilling beyond imagination. He hugged his knees together and smiled to himself almost shyly at the thought of so much victory, such laurels.

There he sat smiling, knocking his heels against the bathtub, now and then getting up and going to the door to put his ear to the broad crack and listening for sounds of the game, the pursuer and the pursued, and then returning to his seat with the dogged determination of the true winner, a breaker of records, a champion.

It grew darker in the shed as the light at the door grew softer, fuzzier, turned to a kind of crumbling yellow pollen that turned to yellow fur, blue fur, grey fur. Evening. Twilight. The sound of water gushing, falling. The scent of earth receiving water, slaking its thirst in great gulps and releasing that green scent of freshness, coolness. Through the crack Ravi saw the long purple shadows of the shed and the garage lying still across the yard. Beyond that, the white walls of the house. The bougainvillaea had lost its lividity, hung in dark bundles that quaked and twittered and seethed with masses of homing sparrows. The lawn was shut off from his view. Could he hear the children's voices? It seemed to him that he could. It seemed to him that he could hear them chanting, singing, laughing. But what about the game? What had happened? Could it be over? How could it when he was still not found?

It then occurred to him that he could have slipped out long ago, dashed across the yard to the veranda and touched the 'den'. It was necessary to do that to win. He had forgotten. He had only remembered the part of hiding and trying to elude the seeker. He had done that so successfully, his success had occupied him so wholly that he had quite forgotten that success had to be clinched by that final dash to victory and the ringing cry of 'Den!'

With a whimper he burst through the crack, fell on his knees, got up and stumbled on stiff, benumbed legs across the shadowy yard, crying heartily by the time he reached the veranda so that when he flung himself at the white pillar and bawled, 'Den! Den! Den!' his voice broke with rage and pity at the disgrace of it all and he felt himself flooded with tears and misery.

Out on the lawn, the children stopped chanting. They all turned to stare at him in amazement. Their faces were pale and triangular in the dusk. The trees and bushes around them stood inky and sepulchral, spilling long shadows across them. They stared, wondering at his reappearance, his passion, his wild animal howling. Their mother rose from her basket chair and came towards him, worried, annoyed, saying, 'Stop it, stop it, Ravi. Don't be a baby. Have you hurt yourself?' Seeing him attended to, the children went back to clasping their hands and chanting 'The grass is green, the rose is red . . .'

But Ravi would not let them. He tore himself out of his mother's grasp and pounded across the lawn into their midst, charging at them with his head lowered so that they scattered in surprise. 'I won, I won, I won,' he bawled, shaking his head so that the big tears flew. 'Raghu didn't find me. I won, I won – '

It took them a minute to grasp what he was saying, even who he was. They had quite forgotten him. Raghu had found all the others long ago. There had been a fight about who was to be It next. It had been so fierce that their mother had emerged from her bath and made them change to another game. Then they had played another and another. Broken mulberries from the tree and eaten them. Helped the driver wash the car when their father returned from work. Helped the gardener water the beds till he roared at them and swore he would complain to their parents. The parents had come out, taken up their positions on the cane chairs. They had begun to play again, sing and chant. All this time no one had remembered Ravi. Having disappeared from the scene, he had disappeared from their minds. Clean.

'Don't be a fool,' Raghu said roughly, pushing him aside, and even Mira said, 'Stop howling, Ravi. If you want to play, you can stand at the end of the line,' and she put him there very firmly.

The game proceeded. Two pairs of arms reached up and met in an arc. The children trooped under it again and again in a lugubrious circle, ducking their heads and intoning

> 'The grass is green,
>   The rose is red;
>   Remember me
> When I am dead, dead, dead, dead . . .'

And the arc of thin arms trembled in the twilight, and the heads were bowed so sadly, and their feet tramped to that melancholy refrain so mournfully, so helplessly, that Ravi could not bear it. He would not follow them, he would not be included in this funereal game. He had wanted victory and triumph – not a funeral. But he had been forgotten, left out and he would not join them now. The ignominy of being forgotten – how could he face it? He felt his heart go heavy and ache inside him unbearably. He lay down full length on the damp grass, crushing his face into it, no longer crying, silenced by a terrible sense of his insignificance.

Can You Hear Silence?

SHASHI DESHPANDE 1986

This story is set in Bombay, one of India's biggest cities. In so many ways it is like any other great metropolis, with its noise and congestion, its bustling traffic and its tall apartment buildings. But every year the spectacular monsoons come, with their great downpours bringing the city almost to a stop – and bringing memories of life in a gentler place.

We've been sitting here and watching the road since the morning. When I woke up, I knew, even without opening my eyes, that it was not like every day. The noises were different. Splashing sounds on the road. A car starting, sputtering and dying away. A funny lap-lap sound as if the sea had come close to us. And above all this, a loud drumming sound. I opened my eyes and it seemed dark. And there was Papa sitting and reading instead of rushing about getting ready. Then I knew what it was.

'Is it raining, Papa? Is the road flooded?'

'Go and have a look,' he said, his eyes still on his page.

It *was* flooded. You couldn't even see the drums round the trees they plant hopefully every year. 'Hey, Rashmi,' I shook her. 'It's flooded. No school for us.'

'Good,' she said and promptly went back to sleep.

Now it is still raining, but not as heavy as it was in the morning. The water on the road has gone down. At the edge of the pavement there is a crooked line of rubbish left by the water. Single torn slippers, bits of paper, flowers, boxes, twigs and all kinds of trash. Even . . . ugh! . . . a dead rat! A crow is pecking at it, daintily, as if trying to choose the tastiest bits. Rashmi shudders when I say that and makes a vomiting face.

'Lunch,' Mummy announces.

'Mummy, you're not going to work!' Chhaya says accusingly, seeing that Mummy is dressed to go out.

'I have to. But after you've had lunch.'

'You promised you wouldn't,' Chhaya says.

'No, I didn't. I said if it kept on raining and if the roads were still flooded, I wouldn't go. I don't have any leave, Chhaya,' Mummy says coaxingly. But Chhaya won't relent and picks angrily at her lunch. I can't eat much, either. I think of the crow and the rat.

As soon as we've had lunch we rush back to watch the road. The door bangs. Mummy has left. She waves to us from the pavement. She looks very small from up here. In a moment, she's lost among all the umbrellas.

With Mummy out of sight, I'm suddenly bored with looking at the road. 'Come on, let's go out and play,' I say to Rashmi.

'No, we can't. We have to wait until Tarabai finishes the clothes.'

Tarabai came late today, and in a worse mood than usual. It was almost like an orchestra, the way she clanged the pots and pans. Mummy hates it, but she didn't say a word. She's a bit scared of Tarabai, we guess. Now Tarabai is banging away at the clothes. Thwack, thwack . . . the sounds come from the bathroom. In a while she comes out muttering angrily to herself and begins pulling yesterday's clothes off the line. She throws them at us. 'Here, do something about them,' she says. They're still damp. Rashmi and I look at them helplessly. Where do we put them up? Tarabai is draping the clothes everywhere, wherever she gets some place, shoving us rudely out of her way as she walks about.

'Tarabai, what about these?' we ask.

'Hang them round your necks,' she says rudely.

I want to retort angrily, but Rashmi stops me. And I remember Mummy's, 'Now, don't fight with her, girls. I need her.'

'Tarabai, why are you so angry?' Chhaya asks.

'What do you want me to do? Sing and dance?' Tarabai says, though not so angrily. She's fond of Chhaya. They have long talks together and Chhaya knows all of Tarabai's problems . . . her drunken husband, her son who's in with the *daruwalas* as she says, her daughter who's sneaking out with boys.

'Can you really sing and dance?' Chhaya asks curiously, while Tarabai goes on mumbling, 'No sleep the whole night, the rain kept pouring in, and I have to start making the *chapatis* at four . . .' She goes on and on while we chivvy her, asking her to hurry up for we want to go out and play.

When she has gone the room looks most peculiar. The curtain which divides the room into two has been pushed aside and instead there is a curtain made up of towels, petticoats and Papa's pyjamas. The fan flaps them into exciting strange shapes. I would like to watch them, but Chhaya says, 'Oooh, I'm feeling cold,' and Rashmi hustles us out.

It's like a Sunday with the corridor full of playing children. Games are already in full swing. Once or twice the dustbin lids fall off with a loud clang as one of us runs round the corner at full speed and bangs into a dustbin. If you don't put the lid back, you get a terrible stink . . . a mixture of stinks, really . . . rotting vegetables, fish and all kinds of queer things. In a little while heads pop out of doors calling children home for tea. Sometimes Panna's mother calls us and asks us to have tea with Panna. We always refuse, but I feel left out when the others go in. Not for the food, really, though to be honest, sometimes it's also the food. Like the day they were frying onion *bhajias* in Vidya's house. I almost died.

Now we rush in too and have our milk and biscuits . . . they're so soggy Chhaya refuses to eat them, the fusspot . . . and go back to play. We're playing hide-and-seek when Mummy comes home. I'm sitting on the floor, my eyes tightly closed, my back against the wall, counting in tens when I hear Chhaya scream, 'Mummy . . .' I open my eyes . . . I'll have to start counting all over again now . . . and there she is, looking down at me with a funny look in her eyes. As if she is both angry and sad. But she only says, 'Why are you sitting there in that filth, Megha? Come on, get up.'

'Auntie, she's the den. Megha, you're cheating. You opened your eyes. Count again.'

'No, that's enough of playing. Come home now.'

As soon as she opens the door, she sees the clothes flapping all over. 'Oh God!' Mummy says. And then, 'Who hung them up?'

'Tarabai . . .'

'Did she expect you to stay in this?'

'No, Mummy, we went out to play as soon as she left.'

She tightens her lips, looks at her watch and says, 'Five hours?'

In a rush she takes off her slippers, flings her bag away, washes her feet and begins rearranging the clothes. Chhaya gets excited and makes a game of it, hiding behind something and saying babyishly, 'Where am I?' Her hands are grimy and she leaves a dirty mark on Papa's pyjamas. Mummy sees it and gives Chhaya a slap. A little one, really. She can't slap like Papa does. But, of course, Papa is rarely home long enough to punish any of us. There are days when Chhaya doesn't even see him. He goes to work before she wakes up and she's asleep by the time he returns.

There was a time when he used to come home much earlier. But then he had a job. 'Now it's my own business,' he told us once. 'And I have to work very hard for a few years. Once I get going, I'll be able to spend more time with you girls.'

'By which time,' Mummy said with a smile that was not really a smile, 'the girls will wonder who you are when they meet you.' Strangely, soon after this, we met Papa on the road and Chhaya didn't recognise him. 'There's Papa,' Rashmi said. 'Where?' Chhaya asked. And even when he came right up to us, she kept saying, 'Where is he? I can't see him.' We laughed at her and told Mummy about it, but she didn't laugh. And that night I heard her speaking angrily to Papa and Papa saying, 'But it's for them. We've got to struggle for some time.' And I heard Mummy say, 'How long? Oh God, how long?'

Now Chhaya cries until Mummy babies her and soothes her. Finally they both lie on Mummy's bed, Chhaya with her thumb in her mouth. Mummy pulls it out, but in it goes again. I look for Mummy's plastic-netted bag that she carries to work. She always brings home something in it . . . vegetables, of course, and biscuits maybe, or *samosas* or puffs or something. Today it is empty.

'Mummy, I'm hungry,' I say. It seems hours since we had our milk.

'Didn't you get anything for us?' Rashmi asks accusingly. Mummy opens her eyes slowly as if she's too tired even for that. 'I forgot,' she says.

We stare silently at her. 'I was too tired,' she adds. We stand glum. Now she smiles . . . and suddenly she looks like Chhaya when she knows she's done wrong . . . and says, 'Why don't you go to the corner shop and get something for yourselves? Take some money from my purse.'

As Rashmi points out some cakes to the boy . . . she's so bossy, she never gives me a chance to choose . . . a man waiting for his change smiles at me. The huge man behind the counter pushes some coins and notes across the glass top. The man pushes back a note and says, 'One bar of chocolate.' The boy brings our cakes and goes for the chocolate. I stand on tiptoe and watch the squiggly little figures as the man makes up our bill. The boy brings the chocolate for the man and Rashmi carefully counts out the money. 'Here, baby, for you,' the man says to me. I'm too surprised to do anything but take the chocolate from him. But Rashmi, picking up the change, turns round instantly, snatches it from my hand, plonks it on the counter and drags me out of the shop. She walks fast without a word until we reach the crossing. As we wait to cross, I look back. The man is going in the other direction. 'He's gone,' I say. Rashmi relaxes her hold on me. The lights turn green. When we're across she says angrily, 'Why did you take the chocolate from him? Don't you know better than that?' I do. Mummy has told us long back . . . don't talk to strangers, don't take anything from them, don't go anywhere with them. 'I didn't take it,' I say defensively. 'I was going to give it back.'

'Taking things from a man!' Rashmi hisses at me. 'Don't you know what men do to girls?'

'Of course I do,' I say with dignity. 'I know everything.'

I know the word, anyway. And I also know it's the most dreadful thing that can happen to a girl.

Rashmi speaks in a more friendly tone now. 'Now, don't go and tell Mummy about it. You know how she fusses. She won't ever let us go anywhere alone.'

I promise. But somehow I blurt it out, after all. We've eaten our cakes and sorted our books for tomorrow. Mummy has put the cooker on for dinner and comes to us for our usual chat. Then I tell her about the man. She says nothing, she only pats Rashmi approvingly. But I know she's going to talk it over with Papa when he comes home. She's waiting for him now. We all are. It's time for him to be home.

But he doesn't come. He's very late today. It's funny how, when you're waiting for someone, the tick tock of the clock becomes louder than usual. That and the sounds of other people's footsteps. Each time we hear footsteps, Mummy sits up and listens intently. But the footsteps go on and she droops again. At last she says, 'Let's talk of something.' 'Mummy, tell us about when you were a girl,' Rashmi and I say. We love to hear stories of her school, her friends and teachers. But today she talks of her home.

'I had a beautiful home,' she says and looks at us with that 'Oh, you poor children' expression on her face. 'It had a tiled roof. Do you know how friendly the rain sounds when it falls on a tiled roof? And how gently it slides off from it on to the ground? It's a steady drip drip that can put you to sleep. Once, I remember, a bird came in sheltering from the rain. It sat in the rafters the whole night. Once or twice I heard it ruffling its feathers. Otherwise it was absolutely silent. And outside, when it rains, the waters run whoosh whoosh in the gutters. We used to wade in them. They were never dirty . . . just twigs and leaves and mud in them.

'Sometimes in summer we slept in the courtyard. We could lie in the dark and watch the stars. And everything was so quiet that when we spoke the words came out soft, as if we were afraid of hurting the silence. The only sounds were the sounds of birds going to bed, or those insects that go on "tik tik"; rarely a frog croaking. Otherwise . . .' She pauses as a bus screeches angrily to a stop. It starts with a roar and goes on again. '. . . there was just silence. I wonder if I'll ever hear silence again,' she says sadly.

'Hear silence? How can you hear silence?' Rashmi asks challengingly.

'You'll know some day . . . if ever you get out of this place.' 'Sounds silly to me, hearing silence,' Rashmi says scornfully.

Rashmi has to be rude to Mummy these days. And if Papa says, 'Now, Rashmi, that's not the way to talk to your mother,' she bursts out with, 'You all hate me. You're all against me,' and stamps out. And Papa says with a sigh, 'Growing pains.' And Mummy says, 'It pains me too.' And Papa laughs. But it's true Rashmi is growing. She won't let Mummy help her to wash her hair, she acts funny with Ravi next door. And she's either sulking or in a temper. Except with her friends, of course. With them she's . . . oh, so jolly!

'You don't even know what silence is do you?' Mummy says pityingly to her. And I think of how our friends yell for us . . . RASHMI . . . MEGHA . . . and we yell back . . . COMING . . .

All this while we've been listening to the footsteps, hoping to hear Papa's among them. There are fewer of them now. Chhaya is almost sleeping. Mummy suddenly rouses herself and says, 'Have your dinner, girls. Chhaya, wake up.' We finish our dinner and still no Papa. Chhaya goes to bed. Rashmi and I argue about whose turn it is to sleep on the 'camel'. That's Papa's word for the hard, slippery sofa on which we sleep on alternate nights. It's my turn today. Rashmi goes to her place near Chhaya, grumbling about how much place she's taken up. I try to make myself comfortable on the 'camel', but the pillow keeps slipping off. I can't sleep, anyway. Why is Papa so late? I can see Mummy is worried. She snaps at Rashmi who's still grumbling. Rashmi pulls her blanket over herself and turns her back to Mummy. Even her back looks angry. But Mummy doesn't notice.

Why is Papa so late? I'm sure now there's been an accident. Suppose he's dead? I imagine all of it and what we'll do and how sorry everyone will be for us. My tummy feels funny as if I have to go to the toilet. I envy Rashmi and Chhaya for being peacefully asleep. I wish I could go to sleep, too, and wake up in the morning to find Papa shaving at the small mirror propped in a corner of the window.

Finally, when I've given up all hope, I hear his step. Mummy gets up instantly. I hear him taking off his shoes, putting away his umbrella. Mummy asks him something. He replies softly as if he's afraid of waking us, but when Mummy goes on his voice gets louder. I close my eyes tight and grow cold. Don't make him angry, Mummy, I plead. It's terrible when he's angry. He doesn't see us, he doesn't look at us, he goes about as if we're all ghosts. And Mummy *does* look like a ghost . . . an angry ghost, that is. As the angry words go on, I pray . . . let it be the kind of quarrel that doesn't last. Sometimes, it doesn't. I wake up in the morning after a quarrel and for a moment there's nothing, then there's me, and the day, and I'm happy. Then I remember the quarrel and the happy feeling goes away. But when I get out of bed, it's all peaceful. There's Papa shaving, squinting at himself in the mirror, whistling when he finishes and going off to wash his shaving things. And Mummy in the kitchen, looking young in her nightdress, her hair in two plaits. She's rushing about, but I can see that it's a kind of happy rushing about, not an angry, holding-herself-in kind of thing. But some days it goes on and on and I feel as if the walls are pressing in on us.

Now their voices are like small, hurting stones. I put my fingers in my ears to keep out the sounds. My wrists and fingers start paining and I remove my fingers. There's silence. But this silence seems even more terrible than the angry voices. Maybe it's better than those whispers, though. The whispers that I sometimes hear from the other side of the curtain. When I hear them I think of what Suchitra in our class had once told me, her eyes gleaming, her face excited in a nasty sort of way. And then I had hated Suchitra and myself and my parents and everyone and I wished I had a room of my very own. Does Rashmi also feel the same? Because one day she said, 'I'm going to sleep in the gallery.'

'Can you sleep standing up?' Papa had asked her laughing. The *gallery* has room only for brooms, brushes, old tins and other junk. But Rashmi had kept on and on, and Papa had said, 'Maybe one day, when we get out of here, you can have your own room . . .'

And Mummy had asked, 'Will we?' And that night I had heard them arguing once again, with Mummy saying, 'No, no.'

I wake up with a start to find that my pillow has slipped off and my neck feels stiff. I grope for it and put it back, wondering . . . is it time to wake up? Then I hear the sounds of running water and I know it's still night. We get water in the taps only at night and Mummy and Papa have to store it up then.

They work in silence. Only occasionally I hear them say something in a husky, middle-of-night voice. Soon the sounds cease. The lights are switched off. And there is silence.

But only in our house. Outside I can hear the trucks rumbling past. From a distance comes the hoot of a train. Soon the milk vans will start. The tramp-tramp of factory workers going to work. People going for milk. The buses. These sounds don't trouble me, though. I'm used to them. They tell me I'm at home in my own bed. And it feels good and comfortable even if I'm on the 'camel'. But just as I'm drifting back into sleep . . . and I must, I've got to get up early to be ready in time for the school bus . . . I see a picture in front of my closed eyes. A house with a tiled roof. The rain falling on it with a soft patter. A bird sitting silent and still. And I think of Mummy's words and wonder . . . can you hear silence? Will I ever hear it one day?

Passage

GEETA DHARMARAJAN 1988

Sometimes, train journeys break up relationships; sometimes they heal them. In this story, we never get to know the names of the Muslim tailor or his wife who decides to leave him. She and their five children take the train from their home, Quilon, on the west coast of the southern state of Kerala, back to her parents in the Tamil Nadu city of Madurai. So a marriage comes to a sad end – except that the tailor decides to travel on the same train, and . . .

The argument has been brief, tedious. During the whole time, the tailor has continued to work his old and sturdy Singer. His feet press the pedal as if the tensile strength of all the six hundred muscles in his body powers them. His face is immobile.

I am leaving, says the tailor's wife. I'll take my chidren and go live with my father, she says. Her eyes glimmer as they catch the early sun.

Go, says the tailor, finally, looking at her for the first time that morning, meeting her eyes with I-dare-you-to-leave eyes. Go, he says again in a voice that grates as if rolled in sand.

She stands there a long while. He doesn't look up as she walks out.

Knowing she will forget, he continues to stitch. The nylon shirt under his bobbing needle takes shape. After nearly fifteen minutes, he opens the small blue door that leads to his two-room house at the back. He bends his head to enter, looks around for his wife, then, whistling softly, he walks back to his machine.

She *is* leaving.

His helpless hands lie still on the seagreen nylon on his machine. He watches a lizard on the painted glass of the ventilator. A primeval creature, bent into itself, bloated with food. Its one leg is half hidden under the point where its tail joins the body. The other legs stretch out and grip. The head is pointed and snakelike. It doesn't move. It hardly breathes. For a long time he sits there, staring.

His dead father comes and sits in the tailor's mind, settling himself on his haunches, prepared for a long stay. I told you, says his dead father. Women and cattle. They are the same. Need to be whipped once in a while.

The tailor stuffs his fingers into his ears.

If you had not been so lenient with her, mutters his mother's ghost. I told you . . .

The tailor sighs.

She's never left him before, not even when each of her five children were born – and now she wants to leave me, says the tailor to his machine.

His mother intrudes. You are the head of the house, she says in her reasonable voice. You're the one who controls everything. She can't act on her anger like this. She can't do that! What right has she to leave you?

She's good. She's borne me four sons. And a daughter, he argues. Children like pearls, each one of them. Diamonds.

Diamonds, jeers his father's voice. Those brats of yours will throw mud on your face if she desires it. She knows it. That's what gives her the impertinence to leave you.

Every time the tailor walks casually into the kitchen for a drink of water from the mud pot in the corner, now for a little oil for his machine, he expects his wife to give in; every time she walks out of the kitchen to collect the clothes of their children, this, that. Once he thinks he's almost won.

His wife is making the rice for the journey. She has to take the day train from Quilon to Madurai, and then a bus to Chinalampatti where her parents live. A ten-hour journey. He'd have spoken his mind but his father is there, squatting inside him, smiling his thin-lipped smile, his mother. His whole village, it seems, has joined them. What can he say to her in front of them?

His wife and children leave at eleven o'clock. He's still in the shop. The children file past. Well-instructed. Shy.

The tailor prowls through the room, loose-limbed and high-strung. She has left bits of herself in the room. He wants to smash something, just as once long ago he'd smashed her head against the ornate leg of the rosewood cot that was part of her dowry. He'd broken her tooth then. He wants to drag her back home by her hair now. Break every limb in her body. He wants . . .

Passing the wash basin, he stops. A strange idea comes into his head. He reaches out for the talcum powder from the crowded shelf that hangs next to the water-stained mirror. He rubs it into the craters of his lean pockmarked face, dusts away the excess powder, gets into his pink pin-striped shirt. He wears his new *dhoti*, white as cooked rice, and puts all the money he has into the pocket of the khaki shorts he wears under the dhoti.

He is all set to travel on the day train to Madurai.

Ai, says his father's voice, a wheezy and weak accompaniment for the tailor, all the way to the railway station. I know you don't even have the sense to listen to me. If you had listened would you be just a tailor now? If you'd been a doctor, God knows you had the brains, would your wife have left you now? Go, go. Do what you like.

He shares space with thirteen others in the cubicle declared to accommodate eight. He doesn't look at the fat Muslim woman with a brood of five children – at least, not as if she is his wife, as she still is though she's leaving him.

For good, she'd said that morning, I'm not coming back to you. Ever. She looks at him as she would a stranger, before looking away.

She seems so different from his wife who loves to travel. I don't have to do anything, see, because I *can't* do anything, she would tell the tailor, always, smiling and showing her broken tooth. Now, her lips are pressed tight. Her bangles are inert on wrists that the tailor can circle with his little finger and thumb, can break if he so desires.

His youngest daughter, her hair newly washed, her thin little body in a blue terrycotton frock that he'd stitched for *Deepavali* – though Deepavali is a Hindu festival of lights and none of his family ever got new clothes for Deepavali, but then, his neighbours were Hindus, his clients, and for days his shop in the bazaar had been studded with a little silk here, a yard of brocade there, and, Please *Abba*, his youngest daughter had begged, Please, and he had stitched the frock for her, in blue terrycotton, her favourite colour, with little tucks that ran down from the shoulders and a lot of lace that she'd loved to wear the first time, and looks pretty wearing now – this his only daughter after four sons smiles at him. She moves her body. She would come and snuggle against him, but there's her mother's hand on her thigh. It must exert pressure. The tailor looks out of the window.

Narial, says a boy, thirteenish, walking up and down the platform outside the tailor's window, selling tender-coconut water. The surge of testosterone that has coaxed a division of cells in the thyroid gland and in the cartilage of the larynx is still at the job of enlarging his voice box. He calls now in a deep, strong voice, now in a woman's treble. He soon comes inside the train and walks up and down the aisle, up and then down, as if the sight of the cool greenish liquid in the tall thick glasses would tempt if paraded closer to the buyers.

Would you like some? the tailor asks his wife. There's an everydayness to his tone. You must be thirsty.

She doesn't even look at him. She stretches out her legs and closes her eyes.

As she sleeps the sari that covers her small bosom rides up. Below the tafetta blouse, the tailor can see her sunk navel, the large expanse of skin stretched tight like a painter's canvas all ready to be worked on, the stretch marks that look like lines of sand dribbled by a schizophrenic kid. The tailor wants to pull the sari into its accustomed modesty.

He stares at the man sitting next to him. That man can't help but see the tailor's wife's nakedness, that man who wears an orange tee-shirt under a white one whose buttons open to halfway down his chest. The tailor glares at him till the man gets up, climbs up to the luggage rack that says clearly FOR LUGGAGE ONLY. He sits cross-legged for a second then stretches out, one leg hilled-up, a palm across his forehead – film-star fashion. Soon he's fast asleep. The tailor's wife has not even stirred.

The train jerks backwards, once, then chugs out behind the huffing steam engine, sluggishly.

All rubber, says the tailor's neighbour, a man in a blue shirt who's been reading a novel with the picture of a murder scene on its cover. So much rubber.

The dark-leaved trees with their slender trunks, their tops crowned with fresh greenness go by in a rush. They have a richness, the sheen of dark silk.

At 1.30 p.m., the tailor's children are hungry. The wife opens her eyes for the first time. She bends down and drags out the cane basket. She takes out a packet of food. All five children troop off to wash their hands at the water-ringed metal basin at the end of their carriage, and troop back.

The eldest boy, a man of few words and nods of the head, disinterested in his family, refuses to share the rectangle of tightly-packed rice that lies on the slatted dark wood of the train's seat. Just a soaked piece of double paper and a *plantain leaf* keep the rice from going through the slats and scattering itself on the heavy iron box of the family tucked under the seat.

The rice looks dry, each grain yellow-brown, tinged with the markings of the spices that have been mixed with it, each fat as a tiny worm. It is hand-pounded rice. Long after the children have dug mouthfuls off it with their fingers, it retains its domed shape wherever it has not been touched.

The eldest boy sits looking at his dusty feet.

Is he not hungry?

The tailor looks at his son. He's just wise. Soon, soon now, he'll ask for food, say he's hungry and the wife will give him a whole packet, the tailor thinks.

That boy will survive, says the voice of his father. He's like me.

Not washing? his wife asks the tailor. Their eyes meet.

When he comes back, his hands washed and water standing in rounded droplets on his new dhoti, the eldest boy is eating. He's got a packet all to himself. The tailor waits, his dark-jointed fingers drumming on the ankle placed on his left thigh, waiting for his son to eat as much as he wants before he can start satisfying his hunger.

The boy eats a little more than half. He hands the packet to his mother, who gestures with a sharp movement of her head in the direction of her husband. He looks shy as he's handing the food to his father.

The tailor leaves a quarter of the rice for his wife, one whole corner of the golden pile. She doesn't eat. She bends to tuck the now-untidy packet into the basket, showing her broad back, an expanse of white tafetta.

Not eating? the tailor wants to ask. He sits a whole moment on the slatted wooden seat, his father opposite him, sneering. He gets up abruptly to go wash his hands.

When he comes back wiping them on a black-bordered kerchief which he then tucks into his rolled-up-to-the-elbow shirt sleeve, the children are heaped around the far window where the vista opens out, unlike the side closest to the tailor where there's a wall of rock and mud, the innards of the hill that had been chomped into for building the railroad tracks. The woman who sat at the far window has moved over and given her seat to them to watch the hills of Rajapalaiyam.

Look, the tailor wants to tell his wife, for she's the one who notices sunsets. The hills look like fine muslin cloth, close-meshed and soft, torn and arranged in overlapping mounds so that where they cross they are darker. Luminous. Translucent.

Tissue-paper collage, says the woman who'd given her seat to the children. It looks like there's a softness there belied by the rocks. They seem to be actually a deep purple. There's an upending swing to her statement.

It's the hot sun, agrees the tailor.

The hills around Chinalampatti look like this too, says the tailor's wife.
You live there?
No. Yes. My father does.
You are going visiting?
Let's say that, says the tailor's wife.
The tailor's heart sings. He looks and looks at his wife till she is forced to look back. He smiles.
The woman traveller gets off at Rajapalaiyam. Others do too. The compartment gets full again. A woman with short squat nails reddened with henna gets on with one daughter, one husband and six pieces of luggage. Every piece is tied in white nylon cloth and, except for a tall, rusted biscuit tin that stands upright and self-importantly, they have a life of their own as they grumble and squeak and settle slowly under the seats. Slowly they collapse into a position of rest. The tailor can barely keep his legs straight because of the tin.
The young man clambers down from the luggage rack. He has to rush to get off. He hadn't told anyone he wanted to get off at Rajapalaiyam. He should have. Someone could have woken him up.
He could have got hurt. Remember that young Hussain who did that getting off a bus? He died, the tailor tells his wife.

It's three more hours to Madurai. Hopefully. The tailor buys the plump and dull purple grapes, the ones that have a thick bitter skin. His wife likes them. He passes the paper cone to her with a nod of his head. *Eat.*
She takes it. She washes the grapes, dipping each small bunch into a stainless steel glass of water, and offers them to the other woman. The woman looks at her daughter. She takes two grapes, hands one to her daughter, rolls the other between fingers and palm as if to clean it, smiles. The tailor's wife smiles at the other's child and hands the packet over to her children.
You eat, the tailor tells his wife.
Later, she says.
Here. He takes some grapes from his daughter, a small bunch, and hands it to his wife.
She is looking at the tailor, willing him to talk to her, say something, anything relevant.
There's a man on the road out there, in silhouette, cycling, pedalling hard,

his back and head bobbing up and down, and, under the grey skies, goats frolic, standing on hind legs to nibble at leaves, feinting at each other. Like jackals intoxicated with honey. Out far away water is gushing out of a pump. Near where it fans out, sprinkling water droplets on all its sides, stands a boy in the pissing mannikin pose that the tailor knows is a famous statue somewhere in some foreign country. He's seen pictures of it in a magazine. Now, he thinks the water pushing from the pump comes from the boy's penis.

He grins. He suddenly wants to ask the woman with the *hennaed* fingers, Do you enjoy sex? Do you want it? Do you like your husband? She and her husband also sit near one another, silent as fighting family members. Do women like their husbands, ever? Do men their wives? But they stay together as man and wife, don't they?

Five children, he tells the other woman. We have five children and we are going to visit their grandparents.

Oh, says the woman.

We may stay there for a few days. I am a tailor and can take some time off, the tailor hears himself say.

Oh.

I have a boy in the shop to help me. He's good. My son here wants to be a doctor.

Oh.

This is my wife, says the tailor, and there's a singing in his head again.

The woman, who wears a perpetual frown and whose lips pout, tries to look friendly.

Do you live in Quilon? she asks.

Well . . . says the tailor's wife, looking at him.

The tailor looks away and out of the window again, past the two girls, one of whom has laid as much of her body as possible on her mother's lap and so looks like a contortionist, a circus artiste caught in limbo, while the other, his daughter, is wedged between her mother's body and the window. He wishes he could just keep going up and down on the train from Quilon to Madurai and back, past the ugly cotton trees with their split pods dangling on weedy branches, stuffed with dirty cotton, past the cashew trees, their fruits red, the nuts underneath withered, through tunnels and past houses of dried grass held down with rope and bamboo poles, just keep going with his family and wife and packed food and money jingling in his pocket to buy a bunch of grapes, a paper screw of peanuts, a few magazines. He doesn't want to get off the train.

The First Party

ATTIA HOSAIN 1963

India is a country in which ancient customs, deeply held religions and radical change constantly interact. What happens when tradition and western progress collide? In this story, a young Muslim woman goes to her first city party and finds that it is an occasion for embarrassment and loneliness in which a moment of kindness reduces her to tears.

After the dimness of the *veranda*, the bewildering brightness of the room made her stumble against the unseen doorstep. Her nervousness edged towards panic, and the darkness seemed a forsaken friend, but her husband was already steadying her into the room.

'My wife,' he said in English, and the alien sounds softened the awareness of this new relationship.

The smiling, tall woman came towards them with outstretched hands and she put her own limply into the other's firm grasp.

'How d'you do?' said the woman.

'How d'you do?' said the fat man beside her.

'I am very well, thank you,' she said in the low voice of an uncertain child repeating a lesson. Her shy glance avoided their eyes.

They turned to her husband, and in the warm current of their friendly ease she stood coldly self-conscious.

'I hope we are not too early,' her husband said.

'Of course not; the others are late. Do sit down.'

She sat on the edge of the big chair, her shoulders drooping, nervously pulling her sari over her head as the weight of its heavy gold embroidery pulled it back.

'What will you drink?' the fat man asked her.

'Nothing, thank you.'

'Cigarette?'

'No, thank you.'

Painting from Bikanar, 1731

Her husband and the tall woman were talking about her, she felt sure. Pinpoints of discomfort pricked her and she smiled to hide them.

The woman held a wineglass in one hand and a cigarette in the other. She wondered how it felt to hold a cigarette with such self-confidence; to flick the ash with such assurance. The woman had long nails, pointed and scarlet. She looked at her own – unpainted, cut carefully short – wondering how anyone could eat, work, wash with those claws dipped in blood. She drew her sari over her hands, covering her rings and bracelets, noticing the other's bare wrists, like a widow's.

'Shy little thing, isn't she, but charming,' said the woman as if soothing a frightened child.

'She'll get over it soon. Give me time,' her husband laughed. She heard him and blushed, wishing to be left unobserved and grateful for the diversion when other guests came in.

She did not know whether she was meant to stand up when they were being introduced, and shifted uneasily in the chair, half rising; but her husband came and stood by her, and by the pressure of his hand on her shoulder she knew she must remain sitting.

She was glad when polite formality ended and they forget her for their drinks, their cigarettes, their talk and laughter. She shrank into her chair, lonely in her strangeness yet dreading approach. She felt curious eyes on her and her discomfort multiplied them. When anyone came and sat by her she smiled in cold defence, uncertainty seeking refuge in silence, and her brief answers crippled conversation. She found the bilingual patchwork distracting, and its pattern, familiar to others, with allusions and references unrelated to her own experiences, was distressingly obscure. Overheard light chatter appealing to her woman's mind brought no relief of understanding. Their different stresses made even talk of dress and appearance sound unfamiliar. She could not understand the importance of relating clothes to time and place and not just occasion; nor their preoccupation with limbs and bodies, which should be covered, and not face and features alone. They made problems about things she took for granted.

Her bright rich clothes and heavy jewellery oppressed her when she saw the simplicity of their clothes. She wished she had not dressed so, even if it was the custom, because no one seemed to care for customs, or even know them, and looked at her as if she were an object on display. Her discomfort changed to uneasy defiance, and she stared at the strange creatures around her. But her swift eyes slipped away in timid shyness if they met another's.

Her husband came at intervals that grew longer with a few gay words, or a friend to whom he proudly presented 'My wife'. She noticed the never-empty glass in his hand, and the smell of his breath, and from shock and distress she turned to disgust and anger. It was wicked, it was sinful to drink, and she could not forgive him.

She could not make herself smile any more but no one noticed and their unconcern soured her anger. She did not want to be disturbed and was tired of the persistent 'Will you have a drink?', 'What will you drink?', 'Sure you won't drink?' It seemed they objected to her not drinking, and she was confused by this reversal of values. She asked for a glass of orange juice and used it as protection, putting it to her lips when anyone came near.

They were eating now, helping themselves from the table by the wall. She did not want to leave her chair, and wondered if it was wrong and they would notice she was not eating. In her confusion she saw a girl coming towards her, carrying a small tray. She sat up stiffly and took the proffered plate with a smile.

'Do help yourself,' the girl said and bent forward. Her light sari slipped from her shoulder and the tight red silk blouse outlined each high breast. She pulled her own sari closer round her, blushing. The girl, unaware, said, 'Try this sandwich, and the olives are good.'

She had never seen an olive before but did not want to admit it, and when she put it in her mouth she wanted to spit it out. When no one was looking, she slipped it under her chair, then felt sure someone had seen her and would find it.

The room closed in on her with its noise and smoke. There was now the added harsh clamour of music from the radiogram. She watched, fascinated, the movement of the machine as it changed records; but she hated the shrieking and moaning and discordant noises it hurled at her. A girl walked up to it and started singing, swaying her hips. The bare flesh of her body showed through the thin net of her drapery below the high line of her short tight bodice.

She felt angry again. The disgusting, shameless hussies, bold and free with men, their clothes adorning nakedness not hiding it, with their painted false mouths, that short hair that looked like the mad woman's whose hair was cropped to stop her pulling it out.

She fed her resentment with every possible fault her mind could seize on, and she tried to deny her lonely unhappiness with contempt and moral passion. These women who were her own kind, yet not so, were wicked, contemptible, grotesque mimics of the foreign ones among them for whom she felt no hatred because from them she expected nothing better.

She wanted to break those records, the noise from which they called music.

A few couples began to dance when they had rolled aside the carpet. She felt a sick horror at the way the men held the women, at the closeness of their bodies, their vulgar suggestive movements. That surely was the extreme limit of what was possible in the presence of others. Her mother had nearly died in childbirth and not moaned lest the men outside hear her voice, and she, her child, had to see this exhibition of . . . her outraged modesty put a leash on her thoughts.

This was an assault on the basic precept by which her convictions were shaped, her life was controlled. Not against touch alone, but sound and sight, had barriers been raised against man's desire.

A man came and asked her to dance and she shrank back in horror, shaking her head. Her husband saw her and called out as he danced, 'Come on, don't be shy; you'll soon learn.'

She felt a flame of anger as she looked at him, and kept on shaking her head until the man left her, surprised by the violence of her refusal. She saw him dancing with another girl and knew they must be talking about her, because they looked towards her and smiled.

She was trembling with the violent complexity of her feelings of anger, hatred, jealousy and bewilderment, when her husband walked up to her and pulled her affectionately by the hand.

'Get up. I'll teach you myself.'

She gripped her chair as she struggled, and the violence of her voice through clenched teeth, 'Leave me alone,' made him drop her hand with shocked surprise as the laughter left his face. She noticed his quick embarrassed glance round the room, then the hard anger of his eyes as he left her without a word. He laughed more gaily when he joined the others, to drown that moment's silence, but it enclosed her in dreary emptiness.

She had been so sure of herself in her contempt and her anger, confident of the righteousness of her beliefs, deep-based on generation-old foundations. When she had seen them being attacked, in her mind they remained indestructible, and her anger had been a sign of faith; but now she saw her husband was one of the destroyers; and yet she knew that above all others was the belief that her life must be one with his. In confusion and despair she was surrounded by ruins.

She longed for the sanctuary of the walled home from which marriage had promised an adventurous escape. Each restricting rule became a guiding stone marking a safe path through unknown dangers.

The tall woman came and sat beside her and with affection put her hand on her head.

'Tired, child?' The compassion of her voice and eyes was unbearable.

She got up and ran to the veranda, put her head against a pillar and wet it with her tears.

The Homecoming

ARUN JOSHI 1975

In 1971, much of the far eastern area of the Indian sub-continent became the independent state of Bangladesh after the Bangladesh Liberation War. A prosperous, middle-class family were proud that their son took part in that war and are even prouder when he returns home to their happy and increasingly wealthy world. But he has just returned from horror and must share it with them – if they will listen.

Since he returned from the war things had not been quite the same. He had fought on the Eastern Front, in Dinajpur, where, he was told, the fighting had been rough. Personally, he did not know. He had been commissioned only the previous year and this had been his first war. He did not quite know what was rough and what was not. It was true, though, that half his men had been killed during the two weeks. Nine had died on the very first night.

The day he returned, his fiancée and his family met him at the station. They embraced, and wept, and, later on, they laughed. His fiancée wore an emerald green sari and in the winter sun, he thought, she looked very pretty. She asked him if the war had been bad. He said it had been all right but he wished so many of his men had not been killed. She said she had been simply dying for him to come back. He said that was very nice of her. Then they talked of the blackouts and the air raids and things they had seen on the TV. By the time they reached home – it was about twenty minutes drive from the station – she was saying that because of staying cooped indoors for so many evenings she had been eating too much and would now have to diet. His mother said dieting gave anaemia. Anaemia, she hinted, was bad for child-bearing.

Now, where he had come from, for days on end, he had not met a man, woman, or child, who had not been hungry; always hungry. Everyone was hungry, once in a way, but to be always hungry, he had seen, was different. It made a bit of an animal of you, he thought, turned you stupid. After the ceasefire he had supervised a relief station. People used to line up two hours in

India Republic Day, 26 January 1994, 44th anniversary of the declaration of a republic, 3 years after independence from Britain.

advance although there was nothing to do except sit and watch the cooks and sniff the air. When they got their ration they swallowed it in about two minutes. After that he could see they were as hungry as before, that in fact they were waiting for the next meal. The old people had not bothered to look for food. If it came their way they ate it. If not, they lay down and died. That was the way it had been where he had come from. So when his fiancée talked of dieting and with what his mother said of anaemia he started to feel a little lost.

His mother was very keen on his marriage. So was he, in a way – until before the war. During the war he had killed ten men, led assaults that ended the lives of many others and had seen several hundred dead, gashed, charred, bloated, hacked, shot through with their hands behind their backs. He had seen bodies gorging the viaducts of canals, flaking off like stale cake. Once he saw a hockey field strewn with the skeletons of boys. That was the first time he had seen dead people, aside from the corpses that he had seen carried around for cremation. His family were well-to-do and there had not yet been a death. So he had not seen a dead body before and now he had seen hundreds of them. And he had been wondering about marriage. What was the meaning of one man's marriage; one man's life? He had been wondering what life was all about. Who, he had been thinking, could possibly be running the world? Such thoughts filled his head with confusion as he sat about or played cards or went out with his father for a game of golf.

He wanted to tell someone about his thoughts. He had no brothers. His father was a businessman. He thought it stupid that he should join the army when the family business was there. His father had donated a lot of soap for the soldiers. He did not make soap. He had bought it from a friend at wholesale. Now he was very busy because he thought a big boom was on the way on account of the heavy demand from the East. He was very busy and he did not have much time for his son.

He had a sister. He used to know her. Now she had changed. He couldn't put his finger on it. But she had changed. She wore strange clothes and shiny chains and goggles. She wore goggles even at night. At times she wore these for riding. She talked strangely, too.

One day she took him to a party. As a rule he didn't go to parties – they depressed him and worked on his nerves – but she said it was a party of young people. He went because he had been having these thoughts and he hoped he could talk them over with someone. Maybe, he thought, he would feel a little better, more at home.

It was a small party. He knew most people. They were the children of businessmen whom he had known all his life. But most of them had changed. The boys had long hair and side-burns and some had beards. A couple of girls were without bras. The others wore pant suits and chains and goggles. All except him smoked. Just before the war ended he had taken in a lot of sulphur dioxide in an artillery barrage and he had been told to keep off smoking for a while. But he could drink. And he drank. All of them talked. In fact they were quite good at it. They could build things up, one on top of another, like children's blocks. One of them said the need was to see things whole, in perspective; to conceptualise. He did not know what that meant but he thought it meant building things up, one upon the other. There was a long-haired boy who had once been in his literature class. Now, he said, he was a poet.

The poet seemed very keen to define genocide. He also wanted everybody to accept his definition. He said it was important to define genocide because how else did one know whether genocide had taken place. He said a great many cruel things had no doubt been done, but it was not correct to say that they amounted to genocide. The things that had happened, he said, did not meet the definition of genocide. Everyone was impressed because the poet said things different from what the press and everyone else had been saying.

They talked about the war and he listened. They talked of the things they had read in newspapers and magazines. He did not know what they had read but a lot of things they said were not quite correct. They mixed up terms. *Bazookas* and mortars, for example, were not the same, nor was an out-flanking manoeuvre the same as a pincer. But everyone seemed keen to use big words.

They also had their own views on how a war was fought. They thought you fought from trenches and with tanks and guns and aeroplanes. They asked him what happened after the tanks and the artillery and the aeroplanes were done with the enemy. He said the enemy was usually still there after they were done. You had to go out and fight him. They didn't seem to believe him.

After dinner everyone was a little groggy. The poet said he would recite a poem.

He read out casually from the back of an envelope but his face wore the death-look. He talked of Golden Bengal bleeding under a violet sky. Everyone became very serious, goggles and all. Some of the girls looked very sad. 'But no matter,' the poet concluded, 'no matter, comrades, you shall not be forgotten, nor your death go unavenged.' He recited something like that.

The death-look still on his face, he asked him if he liked the poem. He said it was fine if that was how it seemed to him. Personally he remembered different things. He remembered, for example, pushing a boat off a bank, under the light of stars, into a pitch-black stream whose name he did not know. He remembered the silhouettes of the six boys in the boat. They had been detailed to demolish a bridge. When he pushed them off the bank he knew they would not come back. So did they. He knew they would be killed before or after the bridge was blown. Whichever way you looked at it, the boys knew, they would not come back. The oldest among them was nineteen. None of them had long hair or beards and none wore the death-look. They just sat quietly, six silhouettes, a little defiant, a little afraid. He said he did not know much about violet skies but he knew it wasn't easy to die. And to die at nineteen – that, he said, was beyond his imagination.

Another time, he said, they walked into a village and there was a child stuck on a bayonet in front of every hut. There was nobody in the village; just a dead child stuck on a bayonet before every hut.

Then there was the schoolful of girls that had been the brothel for a battalion. A battalion, he told them, was a thousand men.

So, he said to the boys, if one were to write poems one would have to get it all in, all of this and much else. And he didn't know what sort of poems could get all of it in.

One day he learnt he had been awarded the *Vir Chakra*. It had been given to him for the night right at the start, the one in which nine of his men had been killed. He had often thought of that night.

He had been told to take an outpost. There had been a lot of shelling and machine-gun fire. Finally, he had ordered a direct assault. There was not much else he could do because they were short of time. They were short of time because beyond the outpost was a highway where a convoy had to be intercepted. He had hoped they would take the enemy by surprise. But as they got within range there was heavy fire from all sides: Brens and machine-guns and a lot of grenades. Some of them were killed at once. Finally, they were in the trenches. There was a bayonet charge and the decisive fight which they had won and for which he had got the Vir Chakra. But that bayonet charge kept troubling him.

At times when you charged with a bayonet it got locked inside the man. You could do things to draw it or you could fire your weapon so that it was released with the recoil. In any case you lost some seconds.

It was quite dark in the trenches. They had not been able to keep a close formation. One of his *subedars* was fighting to the left of him when his bayonet stuck. A soldier moved towards him. He remembered the sheen of moonlight on the soldier's bayonet, pointing towards his belly. The subedar saw it too and saw that he was stuck. He turned, which, in his own defence, he should not have. The subedar tackled the soldier. The next moment he was bayonetted himself. He was one of the nine that were killed.

He had visited the subedar's family. They lived in a mud hut in a circle of mud huts. He had met his mother. She had cried and wanted to touch his hand. Please help us, she had said. You are big people; you can help. The subedar's widow was a little younger than his fiancée. They had two children; two years and nine months. He had recommended an award for the subedar. His children could study free up to college. His widow would get a pension. But he didn't know what she would do. He wondered what a girl did when she got widowed at twenty and couldn't marry again.

While he was on leave these things kept swirling about his head. He lay awake most nights trying to make sense out of things. At times he wished he had a bagful of grenades that, some evening, he could lob, one each, in every doorway down the street; or that there were a war, not a thousand miles away, but right in the heart of their city, in their streets and parks. At other times he was afraid. Dark shapes danced before his eyes and his palms grew moist. What would he do, he wondered, if there were other wars and other bayonet charges and more boys in boats to be pushed into the silence of the night. Sometimes he thought of leaving the Army. Even so, how could he be sure that he would not awake in the middle of the night and not know that somewhere a lieutenant was making a charge, that some subedar, with a wife and children, was getting bayonetted in the moonlight.

But in the morning there were the parties and movies and dancing and the flowers in their garden. There was his sister with her new car, the chains around her waist jangling every time she moved. There were the poets who hadn't seen a gun and arty-arty girls, and charity fêtes and speeches on the radio. There was his mother insisting he marry straight away and, of course, his father getting ready for the boom. He did not know how to fit it all together or whether it could be fitted together. Ever.

The Bell

GITA KRISHNANKUTTY 1975

This story is set in Kerala and describes the traditional life style of a small town in which little ever changes – until one spirited young girl, home from school for the summer holidays, calmly announces that she is going to ring the temple bell. The author wrote this tale to celebrate the actual temple and its surroundings – and, perhaps, to applaud her heroine for daring to be different.

An unusual sense of excitement pervaded her visit to the temple this evening. There had been an argument over lunch, between her and the grown-ups, when she had announced her decision to ring the bell in front of the sanctuary at the hour of *deeparadhana*.

'If Thangam can ring it, so can I,' she debated hotly.

They protested in shocked voices, 'Thangam is the daughter of the temple priest, she is permitted to touch the bell.'

She responded angrily that Thangam came over to play hide-and-seek every afternoon, and behaved no differently from any of them.

'Besides,' she added, goading them deliberately, 'we are all equal in the eyes of God.' She was not quite sure whether they had heard this bit, for they had already turned away in disgust – but, after lunch, she caught them whispering about 'that horrid English school she goes to', which meant that they *had* heard . . .

But she was sure that they had not taken her very seriously. That was the trouble with grown-ups: they always presumed that if they told her that she would understand everything when she was older, she would accept their wisdom and authority unquestioningly and not dream of going against them. Oh well, she would show them, this time . . .

She therefore submitted with good grace to the suggestion that she accompany her grandmother to the *tank* for her evening bath, though she really preferred the makeshift bathroom at the back of the house (it had

Temple at Chengammanad in Kerala

originally been a lumber-room, the old cardboard box that had once held the radio and which was now crammed to bursting with old newspapers, magazines and broken toys had simply been pushed to one side to accommodate a rickety wooden stool, with a *chembu* on top of it to hold the steaming grey water that smelt of smoke). She hated the slippery stone steps of the tank, the dark green slime at their edges menaced her foothold; the water had a sullen, dangerous look, and always felt bitterly cold. But she endured it all today with no complaint, chattering brightly. She did not fuss even when the tiny fishes swarmed around her ankles, pecking at them viciously, threatening her precarious balance.

Back again at the house, she had to undergo the intensely uncomfortable ritual of hairdressing. They smoothed her hair with what felt like a whole jar of oil, separated each shining strand till it hung limp and straight and lifeless down her back, then tied it up in a tight, skin-stretching knot on the top of her head, securing it with a fibre of banana stem. She was thankful none of her school friends could see her like this. Droplets of oil, oozing down her temples, gave her tiny shivers of disgust, the back of her neck felt slimy, made her long to wriggle out of her skin. She bit back her annoyance, contenting herself with a savage swipe at her oily forehead with the edge of her skirt when they were not watching.

She was ready before the evening flurry of lamplighting had started. The old, toothless *major-domo* of the household, Kelu Nair, was instructed to accompany her today. Why could they never understand how ridiculous she felt, being escorted by him? She had reminded her mother many times that she walked alone to school every day, when they were back in the town; that she even went by herself to the bakery at the end of the road to buy sweets and cakes. Her mother simply pretended not to hear. She alternately envied and detested the grown-ups for their loathsome habit of not hearing whatever they found inconvenient to answer.

Sometimes, if she arrived at the strategic blend of authority and appeal, she could induce Kelu Nair to walk a few steps behind her and pretend that he did not belong to her at all. But this was something she rarely achieved. Today he stuck obstinately to her side, imparting bits and pieces of information and advice that she tried to ignore. She quickened her steps as they reached the road, almost breaking into a run. Kelu Nair shouted at her to stop and wait for him. She did not care to explain to any of them that she tried to cover this stretch of road as quickly as possible because the gravel hurt her bare feet. At the temple entrance, she slowed down, grateful for the feel of the sun-warmed stone.

The usual knot of women was gathered around the three-tiered stone lamp at the outer door, talking earnestly in hushed voices, their faces grave and sad. Kelu Nair edged as close to them as he dared. She knew he drank in every whisper that he could distinguish and that he would impart it all, embellished with many scandalous details of his own invention, to her mother and great-grandmother over dinner tonight.

As they started their ritual circling of the outer walls of the temple, she noticed that the football game had already begun on the courtyard beside the sanctuary of *Krishna*. She enjoyed watching the players, particularly since her obvious delight in the vigour of their game, and in the raucously-voiced comments that she was not meant to overhear, irritated Kelu Nair profoundly.

Arriving at the sanctuary of Krishna, she saw that the small door, which the priest must certainly fold himself in two to pass, was, as usual, obstinately closed. Kelu Nair had told her time and time again that the image inside was unimaginably beautiful, much more beautiful than the one at Guruvayoor. She had tried unsuccessfully to discover when he had seen it, since the sanctuary had never been open in her memory. He was extremely evasive on this point, but he insisted that he *had* seen it, and it was oh! so lovely, especially when decorated with *sandal paste* and flowers. Sometimes, when he was annoyed with her, he hinted darkly that perhaps she was not worthy to see it, ever. Today, she circled it hurriedly, her mind full of her secret mission, and almost ran along the long, unbroken northern wall, provoking an incomprehensible torrent of protest from Kelu Nair, who could not keep up with her.

The eastern façade of the temple always enchanted her. When she recalled it afterwards, as she often did, her memories were full of sound and colour. The river ran through here, the jade green of its water melting imperceptibly first into the rice fields beyond and then into the luminous evening sky. In the enclosed area where the women bathed, shrill voices rose above the wet slapping of cloth against stone, the gory details of the calving of someone's black cow dovetailed into a steady drone of devout chanting. A stream of women, young and old, wearing wet, freshly-washed clothes, wringing out their damp hair, flowed from the low, tiled halls. She loved the way the shapes of bodies outlined themselves sharply through the wet, white curtains of fabric hanging about their shoulders. On the other, unsheltered, side of the river, young men dived and swam, slapping each other on their backs, their voices loud, deliberately arrogant. Old men sunned themselves sleepily on the rough, rock-hewn steps leading down to the water. Pigeons whirred and cooed, the big pillared hall on the riverside smelt eternally of their droppings. In the evening sunlight, as they wheeled over the conical *gopuram*, their incredible loveliness clutched at her heart. For an instant she almost forgot her mission – then ran lightly through the hall, over the pigeon droppings, to the tiny temple of *Bhagavati*, perched high on a rock above the river. Standing on the narrow ledge to make her obeisance always exhilarated her: for she felt splendidly isolated here, poised breath-takingly between earth and sky – the bathers in the river were just floating voices, the pigeons wheeled in a sky she could touch with her fingertips.

But the rock beneath her feet was turning cool. She remembered that the hour of deeparadhana was near, and hurried back through the shadow-filled hall. Beyond the tall golden flagpole, tiny pinpoints of light pierced the warm darkness of the inner sanctuary. The first tentative beats of the *edakka* sounded unbelievably pure in a dusk filled with pigeons' wings. She touched the flagpole three times for luck, ran swiftly past the last, the southern, wall, barely turning her head in a hasty obeisance to the *yakshis* beneath the banyan tree, whom she never failed to propitiate, fearfully; Kelu Nair, muttering angrily, was close upon her heels. Rounding the wall, she acknowledged with an involuntary intake of breath the sparkling rectangle of flame that outlined the door of the corner sanctuary of *Ayyappa* . . .

Inside the temple, her feet lovingly caressed the cool stone of the inner courtyard, revelling in its smooth, worn feel. She bowed a perfunctory greeting to the little doll-like *Parvati*, crossed her arms and touched her ears before the dark, almost-invisible *Ganesha*, and came hurriedly upon the crowded main sanctuary. A familiar scent of hot oil and flowers, of *vibhuti* and wet clothes, welcomed her.

The women of the *Namboodiri* household stood in front, in a tight, invisible circle that no one else must touch, their eyes closed, clutching their thatch umbrellas that obscured everyone's vision, their lips moving in an ecstasy of prayer. She edged her way towards them, ignoring Kelu Nair's shocked whispers of protest, almost bumping into one of the ridiculous umbrellas. She saw Thangam standing near the steps, looking remote and rapt with devotion. The rhythm of the edakka was mounting crazily: as the door was flung open, she blinked at the sudden vision of gold. Before she could regret her decision or go back upon it, she elbowed herself quickly through the untouchable circle of Namboodiri women, nearly floundering on the slippery steps. The sight of the big bell above her touched her with a heady excitement. She could distinguish Kelu Nair's frantically-whispered threats, but she reached up, rang the bell with one resounding clang and was down the steps before he realised what was happening.

Dimly, she was aware of dark looks and subdued murmurs pursuing her as she permitted Kelu Nair to drag her away. Returning home in the gathering shadows, his imprecations grew louder and more vehement. Warnings of her great-grandmother's terrible wrath became inextricably mixed up with grim forebodings for her own spiritual salvation. She paid no heed at all, for she felt wondrously light-hearted, excitingly happy. As she climbed over the stone stile to enter the house, she turned for a last look at the temple: it gleamed back at her conspiratorially, blessing her happiness.

She was in dire disgrace. Their tight-lipped silence was infinitely more eloquent than speech, as was the conspicuous absence of her favourite tiny *pappadams* at dinner, the pappadams specially ordered for her every holiday, and served regularly at every meal.

She did not really care. For the silence seemed peopled with a thousand voices singing within her. And she was quite, quite sure that the golden god within the temple, in whose eyes all are equal, had accepted her gesture with love.

The Assignment

SAADAT HASAN MANTO   1949

Translated from Urdu by Khalid Hasan

Amritsar, in the heart of the northern state of Panjab, is the city which contains the most holy building of the Sikh people, the Golden Temple. This story takes place in 1947, when India was divided into India and Pakistan. It describes the conflicts between Sikhs and Muslims and shows how communal loyalties can sever the more generous ties of friendship and gratitude. The author of this story moved to the new country of Pakistan in 1948 and died there.

Beginning with isolated incidents of stabbing, it had now developed into full-scale communal violence, with no holds barred. Even home-made bombs were being used.

The general view in Amritsar was that the riots could not last long. They were seen as no more than a manifestation of temporarily inflamed political passions which were bound to cool down before long. After all, these were not the first communal riots the city had known. There had been so many of them in the past. They never lasted long. The pattern was familiar. Two weeks or so of unrest and then business as usual. On the basis of experience, therefore, the people were quite justified in believing that the current troubles would also run their course in a few days. But this did not happen. They not only continued, but grew in intensity.

Muslims living in Hindu localities began to leave for safer places, and Hindus in Muslim majority areas followed suit. However, everyone saw these adjustments as strictly temporary. The atmosphere would soon be clear of this communal madness, they told themselves.

Retired judge Mian Abdul Hai was absolutely confident that things would return to normal soon, which was why he wasn't worried. He had two children, a boy of eleven and a girl of seventeen. In addition, there was an old

Bhinderanwala, a Sikh leader with his followers, in the Golden Temple, Amritsar,
Panjab

servant who was now pushing seventy. It was a small family. When the troubles started, Mian sahib, being an extra cautious man, stocked up on food . . . just in case. So on one count, at least, there were no worries.

His daughter Sughra was less sure of things. They lived in a three-storey house with a view over almost the entire city. Sughra could not help noticing that, whenever she went on the roof, there were fires raging everywhere. In the beginning, she could hear fire engines rushing past, their bells ringing, but this had now stopped. There were too many fires in too many places.

The nights had become particularly frightening. The sky was always lit by conflagrations like giants spitting out flames. Then there were the slogans which rent the air with terrifying frequency – *Allaho Akbar, Har Har Mahadev.*

Sughra never expressed her fears to her father, because he had declared confidently that there was no cause for anxiety. Everything was going to be fine. Since he was generally always right, she had initially felt reassured.

However, when the power and water supplies were suddenly cut off, she expressed her unease to her father and suggested apologetically that, for a few days at least, they should move to Sharifpura, a Muslim locality, to where many of the old residents had already moved. Mian sahib was adamant: 'You're imagining things. Everything is going to be normal very soon.'

He was wrong. Things went from bad to worse. Before long there was not a single Muslim family to be found in Mian Abdul Hai's locality. Then one day Mian sahib suffered a stroke and was laid up. His son Basharat, who used to spend most of his time playing self-devised games, now stayed glued to his father's bed.

All the shops in the area had been permanently boarded up. Dr Ghulam Hussain's dispensary had been shut for weeks and Sughra had noticed from the roof-top one day that the adjoining clinic of Dr Goranditta Mall was also closed. Mian sahib's condition was getting worse day by day. Sughra was almost at the end of her wits. One day she took Basharat aside and said to him, 'You've got to do something. I know it's not safe to go out, but we must get some help. Our father is very ill.'

The boy went, but came back almost immediately. His face was pale with fear. He had seen a blood-drenched body lying in the street and a group of wild-looking men looting shops. Sughra took the terrified boy in her arms and said a silent prayer, thanking God for his safe return. However, she could not bear her father's suffering. His left side was now completely lifeless. His speech had been impaired and he mostly communicated through gestures, all designed to reassure Sughra that soon all would be well.

It was the month of *Ramadan* and only two days to *Id*. Mian sahib was quite confident that the troubles would be over by then. He was again wrong. A canopy of smoke hung over the city, with fires burning everywhere. At night the silence was shattered by deafening explosions. Sughra and Basharat hadn't slept for days.

Sughra, in any case, couldn't, because of her father's deteriorating condition. Helplessly, she would look at him, then at her young frightened brother and the seventy-year-old servant Akbar, who was useless for all practical purposes. He mostly kept to his bed, coughing and fighting for breath. One day Sughra told him angrily, 'What good are you? Do you realise how ill Mian sahib is? Perhaps you are too lazy to want to help, pretending that you are suffering from acute asthma. There was a time when servants used to sacrifice their lives for their masters.'

Sughra felt very bad afterwards. She had been unnecessarily harsh on the old man. In the evening when she took his food to him in his small room, he was not there. Basharat looked for him all over the house, but he was nowhere to be found. The front door was unlatched. He was gone, perhaps to get some help for Mian sahib. Sughra prayed for his return, but two days passed and he hadn't come back.

It was evening and the festival of Id was now only a day away. She remembered the excitement which used to grip the family on this occasion. She remembered standing on the roof-top, peering into the sky, looking for the Id moon and praying for the clouds to clear. But how different everything was today. The sky was covered in smoke and on distant roofs one could see people looking upwards. Were they trying to catch sight of the new moon or were they watching the fires, she wondered?

She looked up and saw the thin sliver of the moon peeping through a small patch in the sky. She raised her hands in prayer, begging God to make her father well. Basharat, however, was upset that there would be no Id this year.

The night hadn't yet fallen. Sughra had moved her father's bed out of the room onto the *veranda*. She was sprinkling water on the floor to make it cool. Mian sahib was lying there quietly, looking with vacant eyes at the sky where she had seen the moon. Sughra came and sat next to him. He motioned her to get closer. Then he raised his right arm slowly and put it on her head. Tears began to run from Sughra's eyes. Even Mian sahib looked moved. Then with great difficulty he said to her, 'God is merciful. All will be well.'

Suddenly there was a knock on the door. Sughra's heart began to beat violently. She looked at Basharat, whose face had turned white like a sheet of paper. There was another knock. Mian sahib gestured to Sughra to answer it. It must be old Akbar who had come back, she thought. She said to Basharat, 'Answer the door. I'm sure it's Akbar.' Her father shook his head, as if to signal disagreement.

'Then who can it be?' Sughra asked him.

Mian Abdul Hai tried to speak, but before he could do so, Basharat came running in. He was breathless. Taking Sughra aside, he whispered, 'It's a *Sikh*.'

Sughra screamed, 'A Sikh! What does he want?'

'He wants me to open the door.'

Sughra took Basharat in her arms and went and sat on her father's bed, looking at him desolately.

On Mian Abdul Hai's thin, lifeless lips, a faint smile appeared. 'Go and open the door. It is Gurmukh Singh.'

'No, it's someone else,' Basharat said.

Mian sahib turned to Sughra. 'Open the door. It's him.'

Sughra rose. She knew Gurmukh Singh. Her father had once done him a favour. He had been involved in a false legal suit and Mian sahib had acquitted him. That was a long time ago, but every year on the occasion of Id, he would come all the way from his village with a bag of home-made noodles. Mian sahib had told him several times, '*Sardar* sahib, you really are too kind. You shouldn't inconvenience yourself every year.' But Gurmukh Singh would always reply, 'Mian sahib, God has given you everything. This is only a small gift which I bring every year in humble acknowledgement of the kindness you did me once. Even a hundred generations of mine would not be able to repay your favour. May God keep you happy.'

Sughra was reassured. Why hadn't she thought of it in the first place? But why had Basharat said it was someone else? After all, he knew Gurmukh Singh's face from his annual visit.

Sughra went to the front door. There was another knock. Her heart missed a beat. 'Who is it?' she asked in a faint voice.

Basharat whispered to her to look through a small hole in the door.

It wasn't Gurmukh Singh, who was a very old man. This was a young fellow. He knocked again. He was holding a bag in his hand, of the same kind

Gurmukh Singh used to bring.

'Who are you?' she asked, a little more confident now.

'I am Sardar Gurmukh Singh's son Santokh.'

Sughra's fear had suddenly gone. 'What brings you here today?' she asked politely.

'Where is judge sahib?' he asked.

'He is not well,' Sughra answered.

'Oh, I'm sorry,' Santokh Singh said. Then he shifted his bag from one hand to the other. 'These are home-made noodles.' Then after a pause, '*Sardarji* is dead.'

'Dead!'

'Yes, a month ago, but one of the last things he said to me was, "For the last ten years, on the occasion of Id, I have always taken my small gift to judge sahib. After I am gone, it will become your duty." I gave him my word that I would not fail him. I am here today to honour the promise made to my father on his death-bed.'

Sughra was so moved that tears came to her eyes. She opened the door a little. The young man pushed the bag towards her. 'May God rest his soul,' she said.

'Is judge sahib not well?' he asked.

'No.'

'What's wrong?'

'He had a stroke.'

'Had my father been alive, it would have grieved him deeply. He never forgot judge sahib's kindness until his last breath. He used to say, "He is not a man, but a god." May God keep him under his care. Please convey my respects to him.'

He left before Sughra could make up her mind whether or not to ask him to get a doctor.

As Santokh Singh turned the corner, four men, their faces covered with their turbans, moved towards him. Two of them held burning oil torches, the others carried cans of kerosene oil and explosives. One of them asked Santokh, 'Sardarji, have you completed your assignment?'

The young man nodded.

'Should we then proceed with ours?' he asked.

'If you like,' he replied and walked away.

A Trip to the City

MOTI NANDI 1977
Translated from Bengali by Enakshi Chatterjee

For many people, a trip from the simple life of the countryside to one of India's cities remains a dream. A trip to the Bengali city of Calcutta and its sacred river, the Ganga (Ganges), is even more precious. When old Dulal takes his young wife, Giri, from their village on a day's visit to the city, this is supposed to be one of the greatest events of their life together. So it proves to be – but not, perhaps, in all the ways that he had hoped for. Just as the themes of town and country are contrasted, so too are those of old and young, male and female. The story ends with you having to decide about the value of the day's trip to the city.

Dulal, on the wrong side of fifty, had not yet acquired a wife because he had no relatives to take the initiative. He made eighty *rupees* a month by working at a *tailoring house*. Through the efforts of his good neighbours he got married at last to a girl of seventeen from an adjacent village. She had not a soul in the world either, so Dulal tried his best to take good care of her.

He had once promised he would take her on a visit to Calcutta. One day he earned an extra five and decided to take that trip. He took the afternoon off, shaved, blacked his shoes and wore clothes fresh from the laundry. He combed his hair with extra care so that the bald patch wouldn't show; he plucked a few of his grey whiskers. His wife, Giri, wore her best outfit, an old green silk sari she got as a wedding gift from the *pleader's* wife. She wore plastic bangles and green slippers with silver trimmings. She coloured her feet, plaited her hair with red ribbons and wound it tightly in a bun. She took some time to scrub her face with soap.

The shoes were pinching. Moreover Dulal was embarrassed by the looks the neighbourhood boys gave him. He was nervous over the possibility of losing Giribala in the city crowd. As they were leaving, the nurse from the

health centre watched them from her window. She called Giri in, wiped traces of powder from her brow, put a dot on her forehead, and pecked her cheek. 'What a pretty wife you got,' said the nurse from Calcutta. Dulal marched ahead of his wife, a proud man, shoes clop-clopping on the street.

The train was not crowded, though the seats adjoining the windows were occupied. Giri might like to sit by the window, thought Dulal. So he made a polite request to one of the passengers; 'This lady is indisposed; she needs fresh air; could she have this seat, please?'

The man looked up from his newspaper. He gave her a look and moved over a seat. Giri shot an admiring glance at her husband. Dulal felt so elated he made one good resolve instantly. He decided he was not going to smoke a *bidi*, at least for that day.

Getting down at Howrah Station, he held Giri's hand in a tight grip since all sorts of wicked people lurked around. He almost dragged her out of the station. The bridge at Howrah held her spellbound. She let out an involuntary exclamation. Like an emperor parading his wealth, Dulal pointed his finger to a skyscraper on the other bank and proclaimed, 'That building is twenty storeys high. I went up there once.'

That was a lie. Dulal had never been anywhere near it. But seeing the wonder in Giri's eyes as she glanced from building to building Dulal felt nine feet tall himself. He went on with a solemn air, 'These buses are double-deckers. We are going to get into one of those. When we return it will be dark. We'll walk over the bridge. It's a wonderful feeling, you'll see.'

Giri went down the steps of the river and touched the water. She bowed with folded hands. Seeing her do this, Dulal followed. Giri said, 'I wish I had brought a mug or something.'

This amused her husband. 'And go about with a mug in your hand? Don't worry. I'll bring you a pitcher full of water from the Ganges.'

They boarded a bus and went up to the upper deck. Over the bridge, a whiff of breeze fluttered the end of her sari; but Giri, looking pleased, held it tightly. Dulal kept explaining the sights. As soon as they reached Dalhausi, the office area, the crowd swelled. Dulal was in a fix. He didn't know how to get down at Dharamtolla. He was not ready to lead, for fear that Giri may be touched by wicked men behind his back. He tried to push his way through the crowd, but Giri would not budge. The men at the back grew impatient. There were a few irritated comments. Somehow Giri managed to come down the stairs, though she was breathless with embarrassment. The lower deck was worse.

Giri charged ahead, pushing whoever came in her way, and got off. The bus moved away. Dulal found his way blocked by two hands. He shouted as the bus started to move. He was going to jump, but a man pulled him back by his collar, saying, 'You don't want an accident, do you?' The bus sped away. 'But she's all alone,' he said timidly to himself. A tremor went through him. At the next stop, he was virtually thrown out. He began to run, then stopped after a while. He couldn't see Giri in the crowd.

At last he saw her. She was standing, her face half-covered by the end of her dress. Dulal went to her. She stifled a sob and merely looked at him.

'Don't be scared. It's not so easy to get lost here.' Dulal forced a smile.

When they began walking Giri told him that one of her slippers had been left in the bus. This confused her husband. Then he thought, never mind, I'll buy another to complete the pair. As he put the slipper carefully away in his pocket he noticed how small her feet were.

They wandered through the streets till Giri looked fagged out. It was high time they had some rest. Dulal remembered his friend Rai had a tea-shop at the street corner to their left. But he also recalled the loan. He had borrowed two rupees from Rai about five years ago. He never paid him back. Suppose the old man remembered, that could be unpleasant. But he had a brand-new five-rupee note and some small coins with him, so he could pay him back if he wished. Rai must have given him up as a cheat. But he was such a good soul, he might not mind. Besides Giri was with him, that made everything different. The old man might even want to entertain them.

'Ever had a cutlet?' he asked his wife. She shook her head. Good! Dulal thought this trip was worth something after all. 'Come on, we'll have a feed.'

He led her to the restaurant. At the counter he saw a trim-looking young man instead of his friend Rai. It dampened his spirit a good deal. Surely, the old man hasn't sold out, he wondered. He was hesitating when a man with a dusting cloth on his shoulder came out and asked him in.

'Where is Rai? I don't see him around,' Dulal ventured to speak.

'He doesn't come to the shop. His son has been looking after the business for some time. Babu drops in once every evening.'

Well, well – Rai is a shrewd one, he is letting his son learn business. But he comes to find out how things have been in the day. Just like him.

He walked up to the well-dressed chap. 'So you are Rai's son. Glad to know that. I knew you when you were a baby. I am Dulal Manna from Uluberey. Rai and I used to work together in a boarding-house at Sealdah before the war.'

The young man eyed both of them through his glasses with evident disapproval. He paid the balance of money to one of the customers and said dryly, 'Father is not coming today.'

Dulal felt miserable. Should he stage a retreat? The young man asked irritably, 'What do you want to see Father for?'

'Nothing in particular. I make a point of meeting him every time I take a trip to Calcutta. We've known each other for a long time. Rai treats me just like his younger brother. This time I'm coming after quite a while.' He could have gone on but stopped, as the young man was not listening. He was busy with the account book. Dulal stood nonplussed, then crept back to Giri. 'Rai hasn't come in yet. Let's wait outside. We'll go in when he comes.'

They waited further up on the street, away from the shop. A tallish man with a loose shirt who presently walked in seemed to him like Rai. Dulal went up and craned his neck to look. He saw the young man grumble to Rai, who listened with his head hung. It could be no one else but Rai. Dulal was positive. Rai walked slowly out of the shop, his big frame hunched, limbs sticking out like strips of bamboo tied to his body. He used to be so handsome he looked like the *image* of a god. What a fall! He had even lost his mustaches.

'Hello, old man, you've kept me waiting.' Dulal greeted him.

'Oh, hello, how are you?' Rai grabbed his hand, with a broad grin.

'Getting along. What have you done with yourself?'

'What do you expect? Growing old, touched three scores. Health's broken down. But you look wonderful.'

'You know something? I've married,' Dulal confessed with a foolish grin.

Rai stared at him. 'Oh no, not at this age! She's just a baby. Why, Dulal, you were managing fine all these years!'

Looking guilty, Dulal stared at the ground. Then he said apologetically: 'Giribala is a nice girl. Takes good care of me. Giri, *touch your brother-in-law's feet.*'

Giri obeyed. The people in the street looked at them.

Rai blessed her. 'Sorry, I have no place where I can ask you to come in,' he added. 'The shop belongs to my son.'

'That's just as it should be, you need rest. After all you have struggled hard, raising your son. You deserve some rest,' Dulal spoke wisely.

Rai looked over the traffic and said wistfully: 'You know something, Dulal. Angur is dead.'

'You mean her from Baitakkhana?'

'She died of cholera. I tried my best but couldn't save her. Ran into debt also. Two hundred rupees. There was a terrific row at home. Finally, I made peace by transferring the shop to my son. You don't know what the wife is like. Just gives me something to eat and lets me sleep under the roof. Had to leave drinking, too. Can't go begging to the son all the time.' Rai made a pathetic attempt to smile.

'You sound unhappy, old man.'

'It's too humiliating to be insulted by your own son. You won't understand.'

'I borrowed two rupees from you, remember? I have come to pay you back.'

This brought tears to his eyes. 'Now, look at this,' he said hoarsely. 'It's I who should entertain you and now you are paying me back.'

'Don't be formal.' Dulal brought out the five-rupee note. But he must get the change. He had an idea. 'Please wait here, Rai. We'll go and have something. I promised her cutlets. We'll be right back.'

He took his wife in. The man at the counter gave them a nasty look, enough to infuriate Dulal.

'Have you got a place to sit?' he boomed. Giri got a start.

'What do you want?'

'We want to eat.'

They went and sat in a small enclosure. 'Two cutlets. Make sure they are fresh, ' he ordered.

There was a picture of a woman in the wall. Giri was looking down. 'Did you hear him?' he whispered. 'You saw how he treated us. All right, I'll tip the *bearer* four *annas*.'

A cat crept under the table. Its tail touched his feet. Dulal gave it a hard kick.

He gobbled up the cutlets. 'Let's have some chops. A son, indeed! The old man comes begging to him and what a way to talk to one's father. He thinks everybody is a beggar like his father.' The chop was taking time. Dulal howled: 'Where's my chop? Look sharp, man.'

'Stop shouting,' the young man pushed the curtain and looked in. 'They'll have to fry them. It takes time.'

'I don't have any time to waste. Bring me whatever is ready.'

'We have some curry.'

'All right. Some curry then. Be quick.'

As soon as the young man left Dulal whispered to his wife, 'I know how hard Rai worked to keep this business going. Now he has no place here. I'll tip the waiter eight annas. That young man must know his father knew some decent people in his time.'

After finishing the curry Dulal asked for the bill.

'How about tea?'

'No, no, we don't have the time.'

The bill was brought. A look at the amount made him feel empty inside. Giri was intently working at a stray bit of meat fibre stuck between her teeth. She grimaced. Dulal put the five-rupee note on the platter. The man went back to get the change. Dulal made a quick calculation. Two rupees twelve annas. That will leave two rupees and four annas for transport. He won't have anything for Rai.

The man put the bills and the coin before him. He remembered his vow to tip the waiter eight annas. Then he wouldn't even have the train fare. They would have to walk all the way from Calcutta to Uluberey.

Promptly, he put all the money in his pocket. He peeped out. Rai was not to be seen anywhere. He stepped on the street with a merry heart. After he had bought some *sweet betel* he heard Rai shouting from across the street. Dulal turned to stone.

Rai had a vermilion case made of plastic. He gave it to Giri, 'You came all this way and I blessed you without giving anything. Please take this gift.'

Giri looked at Rai with the same wonder with which she had viewed the bridge and the skyscraper. Involuntarily Dulal fished out the rupee notes. 'Here you are, old man.'

'I am going to have a drink after ages, thanks a lot,' Rai breathed in his ears. Then he scampered away.

'I didn't tip the waiter, did I?' Dulal tried to remember.

'I can't say.'

Dulal brought out all the coins and counted. Fifty-three *paise* in all. He returned to the shop. 'Will you please call the waiter who served us? I haven't tipped him.'

He gave him all the coins. The waiter bowed to him in surprise.

Walking on Howrah bridge, Dulal found it hard to breathe. He stood by the railing, facing the dark river. Was everything worth the trouble? Passing trams shook the bridge. Was this huge steel structure going to come down?

He did not want to die. He was a poor fellow; he wanted to live, nevertheless. He wanted to live so much. Giri was all he had.

'How are we going to get back, Giri?' he confided. 'I don't have a penny.'

Giri turned her gaze at him with the same wonder with which she had looked at the bridge and the skyscraper. Then she smiled.

'You know, when the waiter bowed to you, you looked just like a sub-inspector of police,' she said.

They set out on their way.

The Jacana's Tale
The Disciple
The Three Piglets

SUNITI NAMJOSHI 1988

Almost every culture has its tradition of simple stories which contain ironic truths. Some might be very old, such as Aesop's Fables; some are a little more recent, such as the tales of Brer Rabbit. Suniti Namjoshi comes from the state of Maharashtra, in western India. In these modern fables she uses the ancient technique of telling stories as riddles, so that we have no easy answers and will have to find their meaning in the questions that they ask.

The Jacana's Tale

It was still early in the evening, the disciples of the Blue Donkey were gathered about and the Blue Donkey was feeling benevolent; so that when one of the disciples asked eagerly, 'Of all the creatures you have ever met which was the silliest?' and another interrupted, 'No, which was the cleverest?' and a third cried, 'No, no, which was the most modest?' the Blue Donkey paused for a moment and appeared to think before she answered.

'In my youth', she said, 'I was a great traveller and as I was wandering about the banks of the *Ganga* I stopped to drink at a bend in the river. The current was rather sluggish at this point and the water had formed a pool. As I nosed my way through the lily pads and the water hyacinths I heard a voice saying, "But just look at your reflection in these waters for a moment. You are the most beautiful creature I've ever seen." Well, I looked. All I saw was my own face, much the same as usual, and then I realised I had made a mistake and I looked again, this time through the reeds. The voice belonged to a small green frog who was earnestly addressing a large *jacana*. That the frog was caught in the jacana's beak seemed not to disturb either of them. The jacana

Eighteenth-century Mughal painting

was straddled across two lily pads and trying to peer into the water. The frog resumed, "If you put me down, you'll be able to see your reflection much better." As soon as the frog was put down, she dived into the water, calling hastily over her shoulder, "I'll just push aside these pads for you." I had watched the scene in complete silence, but now that the frog was quite safe I ventured to say, "That frog is an astute flatterer." The jacana only looked puzzled, then she walked away a few steps and continued to gaze into the water. At last I realised that the jacana hadn't realised what had happened. "How can anyone be taken in so easily!" I was muttering to myself, when I heard the frog whisper, "But look at her. She is beautiful." I looked. It was true.'

The Blue Donkey had stopped talking. The disciples maintained a respectful silence. Then the boldest of them spoke a little uncertainly. 'Well, obviously the frog was the cleverest and the jacana was the silliest, but which creature was the most modest?'

'Ah,' replied the Blue Donkey smiling benignly, 'I can't tell you that. But consider, there are at least three creatures in the fable.'

The Disciple

One day a tiger came up to the Blue Donkey and said that she was thirsty for knowledge and would the Blue Donkey please give her some.

'No,' replied the Blue Donkey. 'The sorts of things I have to say are not the sort that tigers learn.'

'Oh please,' pleaded the tiger. 'I don't want to learn tigerish things. It's you I admire and I've come to you for Blue Donkey wisdom.'

'You're mistaken,' replied the Blue Donkey, wishing the tiger would go away because as the tiger grew more and more passionate the Blue Donkey became more and more nervous.

'But I've come all this distance,' insisted the tiger. 'You can't just send me away.'

'Yes I can and I do,' replied the Blue Donkey bravely and turned her back, but the tiger began to follow her about. She was a great nuisance. For one thing she made the Blue Donkey's social life impossible. Friends who dropped by would leave quickly. It was something about the tiger's presence; it altered the very nature and tone of conversation. And yet, the tiger herself never said a word.

Soon the Blue Donkey lost patience. Finding herself alone with the tiger, which was happening increasingly, she turned on her. 'Look. You're ruining my life. Please go.'

'But please,' implored the tiger, 'what have I done?'

'It isn't that so much as who you are, and whom you represent and the effect you achieve,' muttered the Blue Donkey.

'But I've told you who I am,' answered the tiger. 'I am your disciple.'

The Blue Donkey saw she was getting nowhere.

'Very well,' she said. 'Come with me then, as my disciple, and we will go among the tigers and convert the others.'

'Oh no,' cried the tiger drawing back. 'That would be foolish and – and quite impossible.'

'Why?' enquired the Blue Donkey.

'Well, because the tigers would eat you, you know.'

'Oh,' murmured the donkey, 'and what about you? Would they eat you too?'

'Oh no,' said the tiger. 'I am, after all, a fellow tiger.'

'Well then, our course is obvious.'

'Is it?' asked the tiger.

'Yes,' declared the Blue Donkey. 'You are the obvious choice for the Blue Donkey's Deputy Among the Tigers. You must go.'

'What? All by myself?'

'Yes.' The Blue Donkey's answer was heartlessly clear.

So the tiger went. What she achieved is still unknown.

The Three Piglets

It was during the days that the Blue Donkey had retired to the forest for a period of solitude. Early one morning as she was trying to meditate she was approached by three piglets.

'Good morning,' they said. 'We've each of us decided what we're going to be, and on the whole we're sure, but we're not absolutely sure, so we'd like you to give us an aptitude test.' They informed her further that the eldest piglet was going to be a poet, the middle one a saint and the youngest was going into business.

'All right,' said the Blue Donkey, glad to be distracted. 'Now, look at me carefully and tell me, please, what you see.'

'I see Wisdom Incarnate,' declared the eldest piglet, smirking a little because she felt she had delivered a poetic answer. The other two looked abashed. What could they possibly say to equal that?

The second piglet pulled herself together. 'I see a blue donkey,' she answered clearly. Then she shrugged. Well, at least she'd been honest.

It was the youngest one's turn, but she seemed to be undergoing a fit of nerves.

The Blue Donkey spoke to her kindly. 'Why do you want to go into business?'

'To pay the bills.'

The Blue Donkey smiled. 'Well,' she said, 'are you ready to hear the results of the test?'

'No,' protested the first two piglets. 'The littlest one hasn't answered yet.'

'Oh yes, of course.' The Blue Donkey turned to the piglet. 'Well, little one, what do you see?'

The youngest piglet looked at the donkey. 'I see you,' she blurted out suddenly, then she looked at the ground.

'Now,' said the Blue Donkey. 'Are you ready?'

'Yes,' cried the first two piglets. 'Did we pass?'

'You all passed,' replied the Blue Donkey. 'But you've got it a bit wrong.'

'What do you mean?' The poetic piglet was highly indignant.

'You, my friend, ought to go into business – or perhaps into politics,' she added thoughtfully. She turned to the second. 'You, on the other hand, might make a poet. At least you try to describe exactly what you see.'

'But what about her?' They pointed to the youngest. 'Will she make a saint?'

'That I don't know,' answered the donkey. 'Saints are beyond me.'

Engine Trouble

R. K. NARAYAN 1943

It does not always pay to gamble – especially when the Big Prize really is big. You could say that this is a tall tale and pure comedy. However, it is also a cautionary one, as the unfortunate winner tries to cope with his prize and the inevitable cycle of events as local bureaucracy starts to get upset about the winner and his massive winnings!

There came down to our town some years ago (said the Talkative Man) a showman owning an institution called the Gaiety Land. Overnight our *Gymkhana Grounds* became resplendent with banners and streamers and coloured lamps. From all over the district crowds poured into the show. Within a week of opening, in gate money alone they collected nearly five hundred rupees a day. Gaiety Land provided us with all sorts of fun and gambling and side-shows. For a couple of *annas* in each booth we could watch anything from performing parrots to crack motor cyclists looping the loop in the Dome of Death. In addition to this there were lotteries and shooting galleries where for an anna you always stood a chance of winning a hundred rupees.

There was a particular corner of the show which was in great favour. Here, for a ticket costing eight annas, you stood a chance of acquiring a variety of articles – pincushions, sewing machines, cameras or even a *road engine*. On one evening they drew a ticket number 1005, and I happened to own the other half of the ticket. Glancing down the list of articles they declared that I became the owner of the road engine! Don't ask me how a road engine came to be included among the prizes. It is more than I can tell you.

I looked stunned. People gathered around and gazed at me as if I were some curious animal. 'Fancy anyone becoming the owner of a road engine!' some persons muttered and giggled.

It was not the sort of prize one could carry home at short notice. I asked the showman if he would help me to transport it. He merely pointed at a notice which decreed that all winners should remove the prizes immediately on drawing and by their own effort. However they had to make an exception in my case. They agreed to keep the engine on the Gymkhana Grounds till the end of their season and then I would have to make my own arrangements to take it out. When I asked the showman if he could find me a driver he just smiled: 'The fellow who brought it here had to be paid a hundred rupees for the job and five rupees a day. I sent him away and made up my mind that if no one was going to draw it, I would just leave it to its fate. I got it down just as a novelty for the show. God! What a bother it has proved!'

'Can't I sell it to some municipality?' I asked innocently. He burst into a laugh. 'As a showman I have enough troubles with municipal people. I would rather keep out of their way . . .'

My friends and well-wishers poured in to congratulate me on my latest acquisition. No one knew precisely how much a road engine would fetch; all the same they felt that there was a lot of money in it. 'Even if you sell it as scrap iron you can make a few thousands,' some of my friends declared. Every day I made a trip to the Gymkhana Grounds to have a look at my engine. I grew very fond of it. I loved its shining brass parts. I stood near it and patted it affectionately, hovered about it, and returned home every day only at the close of the show. I was a poor man. I thought that after all my troubles were coming to an end. How ignorant we are! How little did I guess that my troubles had just begun.

When the showman took down his booths and packed up, I received a notice from the municipality to attend to my road engine. When I went there next day it looked forlorn with no one about. The ground was littered with torn streamers and paper decorations. The showman had moved on, leaving the engine where it stood. It was perfectly safe anywhere!

I left it alone for a few days, not knowing what to do with it. I received a notice from the municipality ordering that the engine should at once be removed from the ground as otherwise they would charge rent for the occupation of the Gymkhana Grounds. After deep thought I consented to pay the rent, and I paid ten rupees a month for the next three months. Dear sirs, I was a poor man. Even the house which I and my wife occupied cost me only four rupees a month. And fancy my paying ten rupees a month for the road engine. It cut into my slender budget, and I had to pledge a jewel or two belonging to my wife! And every day my wife was asking me what I proposed to do with this terrible property of mine and I had no answer to give her. I went up and down the town offering it for sale to all and sundry. Someone suggested that the Secretary of the local Cosmopolitan Club might be interested in it. When I approached him he laughed and asked what he should do with a road engine. 'I'll dispose of it at a concession for you. You have a tennis court to be rolled every morning,' I began, and even before I saw him smile I knew it was a stupid thing to say. Next someone suggested, 'See the Municipal Chairman. He may buy it for the municipality.' With great trepidation I went to the municipal office one day. I buttoned up my coat as I entered the Chairman's room and mentioned my business. I was prepared to give away the engine at a great concession. I started a great harangue on municipal duties, the regime of this chairman, and the importance of owning a road roller – but before I was done with him I knew there was greater chance of my selling it to some child on the roadside for playing with.

I was making myself a bankrupt maintaining this engine in the Gymkhana Grounds. I really hoped some day there would come my way a lump sum to make amends for all this deficit and suffering. Fresh complications arose when a cattle show came in the offing. It was to be held on the grounds. I was given twenty-four hours for getting the thing out of the ground. The show was opening in a week and the advance party was arriving and insisted upon having the engine out of the way. I became desperate; there was not a single person for fifty miles around who knew anything about a road engine. I begged and cringed every passing bus driver to help me; but without use. I even approached the station master to put in a word with the mail engine driver. But the engine driver pointed out that he had his own locomotive to mind and couldn't think of jumping off at a wayside station for anybody's sake. Meanwhile the municipality was pressing me to clear out. I thought it over. I saw the priest of the local temple and managed to gain his sympathy. He offered me the services of his temple elephant. I also engaged fifty *coolies* to push the engine from behind. You may be sure this drained all my resources. The coolies wanted eight annas per head and the temple elephant cost me seven rupees a day and I had to give it one feed. My plan was to take the engine out of the Gymkhana and then down the road to a field half a furlong off. The field was owned by a friend. He would not mind if I kept the engine there for a couple of months, when I could go to Madras and find a customer for it.

I also took into service one Joseph, a dismissed bus-driver who said that although he knew nothing of road rollers he could nevertheless steer one if it was somehow kept in motion.

It was a fine sight: the temple elephant yoked to the engine by means of stout ropes, with fifty determined men pushing it from behind, and my friend Joseph sitting in the driving seat. A huge crowd stood around and watched in great glee. The engine began to move. It seemed to me the greatest moment in my life. When it came out of the Gymkhana and reached the road it began to behave in a strange manner. Instead of going straight down the road it showed a tendency to wobble and move zig-zag. The elephant dragged it one way, Joseph turned the wheel for all he was worth without any idea of where he was going, and fifty men behind it clung to it in every possible manner and pushed it just where they liked. As a result of all this confused dragging the engine ran straight into the opposite compound wall and reduced a good length of it to powder. At this the crowd let out a joyous yell. The elephant, disliking the behaviour of the crowd, trumpeted loudly, strained and snapped its ropes and kicked down a further length of the wall. The fifty men fled in panic, the crowd created a pandemonium. Someone slapped me in the face – it was the owner of the compound wall. The police came on the scene and marched me off.

When I was released from the lock-up I found the following consequences awaiting me: (1) Several yards of *compound* wall to be built by me. (2) Wages of fifty men who ran away. They would not explain how they were entitled to the wages when they had not done their job. (3) Joseph's fee for steering the engine over the wall. (4) Cost of medicine for treating the knee of the temple elephant which had received some injuries while kicking down the wall. Here again the temple authorities would not listen when I pointed out that I didn't engage an elephant to break a wall. (5) Last, but not the least, the demand to move the engine out of its present station.

Sirs, I was a poor man. I really could not find any means of paying these bills. When I went home my wife asked: 'What is this I hear about you everywhere?' I took the opportunity to explain my difficulties. She took it as a hint that I was again asking for her jewels, and she lost her temper and cried that she would write to her father to come and take her away.

I was at my wit's end. People smiled at me when they met me in the streets. I was seriously wondering why I should not run away to my village. I decided to encourage my wife to write to her father and arrange for her exit. Not a soul was going to know what my plans were. I was going to put off my creditors and disappear one fine night.

At this point came an unexpected relief in the shape of a *Swamiji*. One fine evening, under the distinguished patronage of our Municipal Chairman, a show was held in our small town hall. It was a free performance and the hall was packed with people. I sat in the gallery. Spellbound we witnessed the Swamiji's *yogic* feats. He bit off glass tumblers and ate them with contentment; he lay on spike boards; gargled and drank all kinds of acids; licked white-hot iron rods; chewed and swallowed sharp nails; stopped his heartbeat, and buried himself underground. We sat there and watched him in stupefaction. At the end of it all he got up and delivered a speech in which he declared that he was carrying on his master's message to the people in this manner. His performance was the more remarkable because he had nothing to gain by all this extraordinary meal except the satisfaction of serving humanity, and now he said he was coming to the very masterpiece and the last act. He looked at the Municipal Chairman and asked: 'Have you a road engine? I would like to have it driven over my chest.' The chairman looked abashed and felt ashamed to acknowledge that he had none. The Swamiji insisted, 'I *must* have a road engine.'

The Municipal Chairman tried to put him off by saying, 'There is no driver.' The Swamiji replied, 'Don't worry about it. My assistant has been trained to handle any kind of road engine.' At this point I stood up in the gallery and shouted, 'Don't ask him for an engine. Ask me . . .' In a moment I was on the stage and became as important a person as the fire-eater himself. I was pleased with the recognition I now received from all quarters. The Municipal Chairman went into the background.

In return for lending him the engine he would drive it where I wanted. Though I felt inclined to ask for a money contribution I knew it would be useless to expect it from one who was on a missionary work.

Soon the whole gathering was at the compound wall opposite to the Gymkhana. Swamiji's assistant was an expert in handling engines. In a short while my engine stood steaming up proudly. It was a gratifying sight. The Swamiji called for two pillows, placed one near his head and the other at his feet. He gave detailed instructions as to how the engine should be run over him. He made a chalk mark on his chest and said, 'It must go exactly on this; not an inch this way or that.' The engine hissed and waited. The crowd watching the show became suddenly unhappy and morose. This seemed to be a terrible thing to be doing. The Swami lay down on the pillows and said, 'When I say *Om*, drive it on.' He closed his eyes. The crowd watched tensely. I looked at the whole show in absolute rapture – after all, the road engine was going to get on the move.

At this point a police inspector came into the crowd with a brown envelope in his hand. He held up his hand, beckoned to the Swamiji's assistant, and said, 'I am sorry I have to tell you that you can't go on with this. The magistrate has issued an order prohibiting the engine from running over him.' The Swamiji picked himself up. There was a lot of commotion. The Swamiji became indignant. 'I have done it in hundreds of places already and nobody questioned me about it. Nobody can stop me from doing what I like – it's my master's order to demonstrate the power of the *Yoga* to the people of this country, and who can question me?'

'A magistrate can,' said the police inspector, and held up the order. 'What business is it of yours or his to interfere in this manner?' 'I don't know all that; this is his order. He permits you to do everything except swallow potassium cyanide and run this engine over your chest. You are free to do whatever you like outside our jurisdiction.'

'I am leaving this cursed place this very minute,' the Swamiji said in great rage, and started to go, followed by his assistant. I gripped his assistant's arm and said, 'You have steamed it up. Why not take it over to that field and then go.' He glared at me, shook off my hand and muttered, 'With my *Guru* so unhappy, how dare you ask me to drive?' He went away. I muttered, 'You can't drive it except over his chest, I suppose?'

I made preparations to leave the town in a couple of days, leaving the engine to its fate, with all its commitments. However, Nature came to my rescue in an unexpected manner. You may have heard of the earthquake of that year which destroyed whole towns in Northern India. There was a reverberation of it in our town, too. We were thrown out of our beds that night, and doors and windows rattled.

Next morning I went over to take a last look at my engine before leaving the town. I could hardly believe my eyes. The engine was not there. I looked about and raised a hue and cry. Search parties went round. And the engine was found in a disused well near by, with its back up. I prayed to heaven to save me from fresh complications. But the owner of the house, when he came round and saw what had happened, laughed heartily and beamed at me: 'You have done me a service. It was the dirtiest water on earth in that well and the municipality was sending notice to close it, week after week. I was dreading the cost of closing, but your engine fits it like a cork. Just leave it there.'

'But, but . . .'

'There are no buts. I will withdraw all complaints and charges against you, and build that broken wall myself, but only leave the thing there.'

'That's hardly enough.' I mentioned a few other expenses that this engine had brought on me. He agreed to pay for all that.

When I again passed that way some months later I peeped over the wall. I found the mouth of the well neatly cemented up. I heaved a sigh of great relief.

The Homecoming

MRINAL PANDE 1970

Translated from Hindi by Mrinal Pande

> This story is set in Almora, in the foothills of the Himalayas in northern Uttar Pradesh. Even in summer, with its daytime heat, the nights can be cold. In this tale, the young man who visits his old grandmother comes to realise how each generation must cope with sometimes bitter social and economic changes. Her realistic acceptance of change and loss, even in family relationships, is a lesson that he learns and respects.

The pebble sank in the water with a tiny splash. Hordes of gnats immediately rose from the tank with a sleepy whine and then settled down again. The water looked the same now – a bright oily green, smelly, and glowing with a redness where the old bougainvillaea branches drooped over it. Beyond the tank the house lay criss-crossed with shadows. Except for a pair of doves cooing somewhere in the orchard, it was all so quiet that one felt it was a make-believe world, created momentarily by the shadows. He shivered and found that the day was nearly over. He had quite forgotten how short the days are, here in the hills.

'Would you like some tea now?' The little servant boy stood squinting at him. His light brown eyes darted around quickly taking in everything.

'Be a little careful with your wallet and things, I'm not quite sure that this boy . . .' Grandmother had left the sentence unfinished. He was looking for a comfortable angle in the old armchair, feeling the curves with his back. He paused and looked at her questioningly, but she had fallen silent again. They sat wrapped up in a warm homely lethargy, the silence purring between them like a soft and contented cat. He shook himself gently and peered outside as the municipal clock struck two. A sparrow was examining him gravely, her head tilted a little. She flew away as he pushed the chair back and stood up. Grandmother did not stir, perhaps she had fallen asleep.

He came out into the courtyard downstairs. The large slates of stone that paved it had cracked in many places. There were little blades of grass peeping out through the holes. When they were children they had played *baghbakri* and hopscotch on those stone tiles so often, drawing the lines and squares with bits of chalk they stole from their classrooms. He saw a little white line and went closer. Could it . . .? It turned out to be bird droppings. He began to laugh. How could the courtyard stones have retained those lines after so many years? Actually when you counted the years since then, it really was so very long, wasn't it? He felt unaccountably sad.

The tap near the tank was leaking, the drops fell into the water with a musical continuity. He began to feel soothed and sleepy. Between him and the hills in front lay a vast stretch of ugly wooden structures with rusty tin roofs and backyards full of dirty laundry. The wind felt colder now, the shadows were lengthening across the tiles. He went and stood near the tank and threw a stone into it. The gnats flew up again . . .

Tiluwa the servant boy, having delivered his invitation to tea, bent over the ledge and yelled to his cronies somewhere down below to keep his turn for him, he would be back with them soon.

Without realising it, he had hunched his shoulders a little against the cutting breeze. The house had now begun to look even more dilapidated and old. The sunlight having moved away, the shadows had brought out its true age with all its hideous details: the broken tin pipes hanging from the eaves, the creaky wooden veranda upstairs, the cracked tiles. He thought he should warn Grandmother about all this. Perhaps right now it could be ignored, but when the cold winter storms come hurtling down here from the Tibetan plateaus, the house was not going to be a very safe place to live in. He moved away from the smelly tank. Tiluwa had disappeared. He checked his room. His suitcase was locked, his wallet was in his pocket. Reassured, he went upstairs.

Grandmother was sitting up in her bed with a blanket over her knees. There was a little table next to her bed with the tea things on it. He sat down. Grandmother pushed a large brass tumbler towards him. 'See if the sugar is enough for you.'

He picked up the hot tumbler gingerly and sipped the tea. The brew was scalding hot and very sweet. It had a mild smoky flavour that he didn't quite dislike. 'It's fine,' he smiled at her.

She was sipping her own tea and peering at him closely. 'Tell me about yourself. You seem to have lost weight.'

He put his tumbler down and picked up a salty cracker from the plate. 'You tell me about yourself first. How have you been keeping these days?'

'I get along. If the pain gets too bad, I get my knees massaged with warm oil. Here, try this sweet mango pickle.' She pushed the bowl towards him.

He felt that she was a little reluctant to speak about herself. Perhaps then he should not ask her such questions. 'Can you get raw mangoes in these hills?'

'You don't get the pickling variety here normally, but Bhawanidutt, the shopkeeper, got me some from the plains this summer.'

'Is that so?' He felt somewhat silly at having spoken at all. Her silence made him feel as if he were loud, gaudy, gauche. After a while he cleared his throat. 'Don't you make the sweet lemon pickle any more?'

She was wiping her glasses with the edge of her shawl. She paused. Her eyes were closed, so he could not make out the expression in them, but noticed for the first time that even her eyebrows had turned a snowy white. How old was she? Seventy-five? Eighty, perhaps.

'The lemon trees were sold off with the orchard and the guest house.' Her tone was as flat as though she was discussing someone else's property. He remembered the family discussing the deal and bargaining for a little more from the buyer. He felt ashamed for having asked about it at all. Grandmother used to be so proud of that grove of lemon trees. Each year, as soon as the little green shapes of the lemons emerged on the branches, she would start planning to make preserves and cordials. When the servants went with sacks to fetch the fruit, she'd stand there and supervise the job herself: 'Be careful! Don't break the branches, you'll bruise the tree.'

He sat silent for a while with his eyes lowered. 'Who bought them?'

'There's a new *Panjabi* settler.' Her voice lacked anger or accusation. 'It's all right, really. I used to make all those preserves only for you people. What would I do with the fruit now? Hey, Tiluwa!'

He began sipping his tea again.

Tiluwa stood at the door, an insolent smile on his face. 'What do you want me to do now? Get the vegetables?' The boy had probably had to leave his game half-finished. He felt his own face flush with sudden anger at the sound of Tiluwa's young and rude voice. He wished he could slap the smile off the boy's snotty face. *Sala!* Why couldn't he stand straight?

Grandmother's face remained impassive. Perhaps she was used to all this. She fumbled under her pillow and took out an old *zari* purse and from it a crumpled-looking five-rupee note. She held it out to him. 'See if this is a five-rupee one?' He nodded in confirmation. She extended her hand towards Tiluwa. 'Here, ask Bhawanidutt to give you fresh ones. Don't lose the money, do you hear me? Tuck it into your pocket properly, and don't start playing games in the street on your way home. Come back soon!'

Tiluwa almost snatched the money from her hand and went out like a whirlwind into the street with a great banging of doors and scraping of feet. Grandmother began telling him anxiously how this orphaned boy had come begging at her door one day and how she had kept him in her employ since then. 'He has a stepmother he does not wish to go back to, but here these streetboys make very bad company. How long does it take for a young boy to get into mischief, after all?'

He listened quietly, politely nodding in agreement. Her little wrinkled hands lay in her lap. He found the pose almost unbearably defenceless. They sat quiet for a long while listening to the windy noises growing louder outside. He felt the lights grow dimmer. Perhaps it was just growing darker and the bulbs were too dusty. The tin sheets on the roof made peculiar noises as they contracted with the chill. It sounded almost as though someone was walking overhead. Ancestral footfalls? He shivered and looked around trying to compose himself. Everything in the room had been in the same spot all these years: the bookshelves, the arm chairs, the *images* of family gods sitting in a semi-circle on the large silver platter. Everything cast even larger and weirder shadows upon the dim walls. He wanted a smoke badly but how could he smoke in front of her? He gave a start at the sound of her voice. 'Go ahead and smoke if you want to; it's all right with me.' He felt a little awed. Perhaps one's extra-sensory perceptions grew sharper in seclusion, like those of yogas living in mountain caves. He glanced at her out of the corners of his eyes. She had closed her eyes and lay back upon the pillows. He lit his cigarette.

'They were all just as shy about it when they smoked. All of them smoked and thought I didn't know that they did.' She smiled faintly. Her hands were playing with her glasses. He felt his stomach contract slightly. At last the subject had been broached that he had been trying to avoid all this while. He just could not bear to face the ugly revelations of their collective guilt that were about to surface. But she spoke no further; her face indeed seemed half-shut – if one may use that adjective for a face, that is. He suddenly realised that for her the act of remembering her children was no longer evoking the personal grudges connected with them. It was just naming them with detachment and wonder, just as she remembered the lemon trees that had belonged to her once. But then perhaps he was just imagining all this, to assuage his own part in the collective guilt. Was it really so easy to detach oneself totally from one's own flesh and blood and become entirely self-contained?

'The house has begun to feel quite old, hasn't it?' He looked around for an ashtray and finally put the butt into the tumbler in front of him. There was a faint sizzle. 'You said something?' Her face turned to him slowly. The wind banged the broken pipes against the tin roof outside. It sounded like a sinister pendulum sounding away the hours.

'Nothing.' He fell silent.

There was some noise in the kitchen now. 'Is that you, Tiluwa?' she enquired. Tiluwa's head appeared around the door. 'I got *brinjals*, spinach and green beans. Everything else was sold out already.' A hand was thrust forward towards them with a bag that presumably held the purchases.

'Look, get the small charcoal *sigri* going and cook the brinjals and green beans for *Babuji's* dinner. And make some *parathas*. Go easy on the salt though, understand?' Tiluwa mumbled that he'd never ever been known to over-season anything so why should he do it now, and disappeared again.

For some time he listened to the boy pottering around in the kitchen singing film songs. Grandmother lowered the pillows and stretched out her legs. Her face contorted with pain for a brief spell. 'Hey, *Ram!*' He tried to say something, but couldn't. What could he have said, anyhow? The pipes banged against the roof outside again.

'The pipes need to be changed.' He took out another cigarette and then put it back again. There were only two left in the pack. He'd need them more in the morning. God knows if one could get cigarettes in this little town at this hour.

'What? Oh the pipes. Well, I had a rough estimate prepared and it seems that the prices have risen twentyfold at least. Everything costs so much more than one can possibly pay. And then, the quality of things is always suspect. What is the use? I refuse to have the repairs done at those prices.'

'But how much longer can it last like this?'

The hollowness of the question stung him with shame as soon as he had asked it.

'As long as He wills it to. As for me, a single room is enough. So why bother?' Her voice was toneless. They sat quietly for what seemed ages, until Tiluwa peeked in through the door.

'Food? Bring it here.' She propped herself up against the pillows. 'And take these tumblers away, they've been lying around for hours.'

The food tasted of unskilled hands.

'Is it cooked properly?' she asked. She ate only once a day, in the mornings, he remembered.

'Yes.' He paused. 'Won't you have your glass of milk, at least?'

'No, it gives me flatulence now.' Again she avoided discussing her health.

Tiluwa took the platter away. He washed his hands under the freezing cold tap outside. When he came back, she held out her tiny palm towards him. It held a few *cardamoms*. He picked one up and sat down again. Tiluwa was making a great deal of noise in the kitchen, scrubbing pots and singing the while.

'How long have you come for this time?'

'I have to go back tomorrow, actually . . .'

He cast about for a suitable explanation, but Grandmother merely lay down again with closed eyes. No, he did not need one, really.

'What time do you have to leave?' The enquiry was free of sarcasm or anger, he was relieved to note.

'Seven thirty or so.'

'Tiluwa will wake you up at six then.' She smoothed the creases on her pillowcase. 'Go to sleep now or you will be tired tomorrow.'

He stood up. 'Shall I put out the light?'

'No, Tiluwa can do that. He has to give me back the keys before he goes to sleep.' She had closed her eyes again. He left the room.

The wiring downstairs had probably not been checked for a long time. There were no bulbs in the light fittings either. Tiluwa had placed an old kerosene lamp with a soot-covered chimney on the table next to his bed. He raised it a little and peered around. The room reeked of neglect and disuse. The clean sheets on the bed and his crisp white clothes seemed out of place there. In a corner, there was an old tin box covered with dust and cobwebs. He opened it. It was full of old phonograph records from another era − Angurbala, Janakibai, Gulab Jan. The covers crumbled to dust between his fingertips. There was also a tiny box full of old phonograph needles that looked like sawn-off sewing-machine needles. The phonograph itself had disappeared. So had all the books from the old shelves that lined the walls, covered with dust. There were just some stacks of old magazines in a corner, all dusty and crumbling with age. He remembered the family complaining angrily that people had carried away everything of value from the downstairs portion of the house and that no one had ever checked them. He could not remember now whether the anger had been directed more against the loss of property or against the person or persons who had failed to prevent it.

He tossed in his bed. The storm outside had subsided. All that remained now was the gentle murmur of the leaves and the soft sound of the drops falling into the tank from that leaky tap. Strange, he thought, how irrevocable is the slow decadence of old family ties! It seemed as though he lay in a room in some old and unknown wayside inn. There was nothing, absolutely nothing here that he could connect himself to and feel that he was home.

In the morning he climbed upstairs, his feet dragging a little. He had not slept too well and his head hurt. She was doing the *arti*, muttering the words of prayer slowly. As she stood up, the morning light showed her bent back and the grey in her face even more clearly.

'I made *puris* for you, as it is too early to eat a big meal.' He was about to say that there was no need for all that, but he quietly swallowed his words. They sat down. Tiluwa brought a *thali* full of puris and spiced potato curry. 'It's too much,' he said. Grandmother asked Tiluwa to bring a smaller plate so that Babuji could put aside what he did not need. He said the food was very good.

'I doubt it.' She sipped her tea slowly. 'All that one does now is to pay a lot of money for mere trifles and inferior goods. You can get neither the same spices that we used to, nor the *ghee*. What is the point of making festive foods anymore? Times being what they are, people can't digest them anyway.'

He took a large swallow of water. He did not quite know what to say. When he had finished his meal and washed his hands, he found her sitting in a chair with a small plate of rice and *kumkum* in her lap. 'I find it hard to stand up often. Will you bend down, just a little? I'll put a *tilak* on you. There . . .' She thrust some money into his hands. He felt strange accepting money from her. She sensed his hesitation. 'Keep it. It's just for good luck, and it's not much, anyhow. Tiluwa! Go and put Babuji's luggage in the car.'

Tiluwa went leaping down the stairs two steps at a time. After that the room fell silent again. Grandmother sat looking at a long beam of sunlight on the threshold. He touched her feet. 'Well then.'

'Bless you, son.'

Neither of them said any more. As he turned around at the bottom of the stairs for a final farewell, he found her sitting still with her eyes fixed upon the little island of sun upon the threshold. He was about to wave goodbye to her but dropped his hand quietly. She had said her farewell already.

January Night

PREMCHAND (DHANPAT RAI SRIVASTVA) 1930
Translated from Hindi by David Rubin

What do you do when you are desperately poor? The famous Hindi author, Premchand, sets his tale in the nothern state of Uttar Pradesh. His hero, the peasant Halku, has at least the consolation of his dignity as a tenant farmer, even though he would be better off as a farm labourer. But one January night the greed of the landowner, the bitter cold and fate combine to deal him a tragedy from which he cannot escape.

Halku came in and said to his wife, 'The landlord's come. Get the *rupees* you set aside. I'll give him the money and somehow or other we'll get along without it.'

Munni had been sweeping. She turned around and said, 'But there are only three rupees. If you give them to him, where's the blanket going to come from? How are you going to get through these January nights in the fields? Tell him we'll pay him after the harvest, not right now.'

For a moment, Halku stood hesitating. January was on top of them. Without a blanket, he could not possibly sleep in the fields at night. But the landlord would not be put off; he'd threaten and insult him. So what did it matter if they died in the cold weather as long as they could just take care of this calamity right now? As he thought this, he moved his heavy body that gave the lie to his name and came close to his wife. Trying to coax her, he said, 'Come on, give it to me. We'll manage. I'll figure out some other plan to get the blanket.'

Munni drew away from him. Her eyes angry, she said, 'You've already tried "Some other plan". You just tell me what other plan can be found. Is somebody going to give you a blanket? God knows how many debts are always left over that we can't pay off. What I say is, give up this tenant

farming. The work's killing you. Whatever you harvest goes to pay up the arrears, so why not finish with it? Were we born just to keep paying off debts? Earn some money for your own belly, give up that kind of farming. I won't give you the money, I won't!'

Sadly Halku said, 'Then I'll have to put up with his abuse.'

Losing her temper, Munni said, 'Why should he abuse you – is this his kingdom?'

But as she said it, her brows relaxed from the frown. The bitter truth in Halku's words came charging at her like a wild beast.

She went to the niche in the wall, took out the rupees and handed them over to Halku. Then she said, 'Give up farming this time. If you work as a hired labourer you'll get enough food to eat from it. No one will be yelling insults at you. Fine work, farming someone else's land! Whatever you earn you throw back into it and get insulted into the bargain.'

Halku took the money and went outside looking as though he were tearing his heart out and giving it away. He'd saved the rupees from his work, *pice* by pice, for his blanket. Today he was going to throw it away. With every step, his head sank lower under the burden of his poverty.

2

A dark January night. In the sky, even the stars seemed to be shivering. At the edge of his field, underneath a shelter of cane leaves, Halku lay on a bamboo *cot* wrapped up in his old sacking, shivering. Underneath the cot his friend, Jabra the dog, was whimpering with his muzzle pressed into his belly. Neither one of them was able to sleep. Halku curled up, drawing his knees close against his chin, and said, 'Cold, Jabra? Didn't I tell you in the house you could lie in the *paddy* straw? So why did you come out here? Now you'll have to bear the cold, there's nothing I can do. You thought I was coming out here to eat *puris* and sweets and came running ahead of me. Now you can moan all you want.'

Jabra wagged his tail without getting up, protracted his whimpering into a long yawn and was silent. Perhaps in his canine wisdom he guessed that his whimpering was keeping his master awake.

Halku reached out his hand and patted Jabra's cold back. 'From tomorrow on, stop coming with me or the cold'll get you. This bitch of a west wind comes from nobody-knows-where, bringing the icy cold with it. Let me get up and fill my pipe. I've smoked eight pipefuls already but we'll get through the night somehow. This is the reward you get for farming. Some lucky fellows are lying in houses where if the cold comes the heat just drives it away. A good thick quilt, warm covers, blankets! Just let the winter cold try to get them! Fortune's arranged everything very well. While we do the hard work somebody else gets the joy of it.'

He got up, took some embers from the pit and filled his pipe. Jabra got up too.

Smoking, Halku said, 'If you smoke, the cold's just as bad but at least you feel better.'

Jabra looked at him with eyes overflowing with love.

'You've got to put up with just one more cold night. Tomorrow I'll spread some straw. When you bed down in that you won't feel the cold.'

Jabra put his paws on Halku's knees and brought his muzzle close. Halku felt his warm breath. After he finished smoking, Halku lay down and made up his mind that, however bad things were, he would sleep now. But in only one minute his heart began to pound. He turned from side to side. Like some kind of witch, the cold weather continued to torment him. When he could bear it no longer, he gently picked Jabra up and, patting his head, got him to fall asleep in his lap. The dog's body gave off some kind of stench but Halku, hugging him tight, experienced a happiness he had not felt for months. Jabra probably thought he was in heaven, and in Halku's innocent heart there was no resentment of his smell. He embraced him with the very same affection he would have felt for a brother or a friend. He was not crippled by the poverty which had reduced him to these straits at present. Rather, it was as though this singular friendship had opened all the doors to his heart and brilliantly illuminated every atom of it.

Suddenly, Jabra picked up the noise of some animal. This special intimacy had produced a new alertness in him that disdained the onslaught of the wind. Springing up, he ran out of the shelter and began to bark. Halku whistled and called him several times. But Jabra would not come back to him. He went on barking while he ran around through the furrows of the field. He would come back for a moment, then dash off again at once. The sense of duty had taken possession of him as though it were desire.

Another hour passed. The night fanned up the cold with the wind. Halku sat up and, bringing both knees tight against his chest, hid his face between them but the cold was just as biting. It seemed as though all his blood had frozen, that ice rather than blood filled his veins. He leaned back to look at the skies. How much of the night was still left! The *Dipper* had not yet climbed half the sky. By the time it was overhead it would probably be morning. Night would last another three hours or so.

Only a stone's throw from Halku's field there was a mango grove. The leaves had begun to fall and they were heaped up in the grove. Halku thought, 'If I go and get a pile of leaves I can make a fire and keep warm. If anybody sees me gathering the leaves in the dead of night they'll think it's a ghost. Of course there's a chance some animal's hidden in my field waiting, but I can't put up with sitting here any longer.' He ripped up some stalks from a nearby field, made a broom out of them and, picking up a lighted cowdung cake, went towards the grove. Jabra watched him coming and ran to him, wagging his tail.

Halku said, 'I couldn't stand it any more, Jabra. Come along, let's go into the orchard and gather leaves to warm up with. When we're toasted, we'll come back and sleep. The night's still far from over.'

Jabra barked his agreement and trotted on towards the orchard. Under the trees it was pitch dark and in the darkness the bitter wind blew, buffeting the leaves, and drops of dew dripped from the branches. Suddenly, a gust carried the scent of *henna blossom* to him. 'Where's that sweet smell coming from, Jabra? Or can't your nose make out anything as fragrant as this?'

Jabra had found a bone lying somewhere and he was chewing on it. Halku set his fire down on the ground and began to gather the leaves. In a little while, he had a great heap. His hands were frozen, his bare feet numb. But he'd piled up a regular mountain of leaves and by making a fire out of them he would burn away the cold. In a little while, the fire was burning merrily. The flames leapt upward, licking at the overhanging branches. In the flickering light, the immense trees of the grove looked as though they were carrying the vast darkness on their heads. In the blissful sea of darkness, the firelight seemed to pitch and toss like a boat.

Halku sat before the fire and let it warm him. After a while, he took off his shawl and tucked it behind him, then he spread out both feet as though challenging the cold to do its worst. Victorious over the immense power of winter, he could not repress his pride in his triumph. He said to Jabra, 'Well, Jabra, you're not cold now, are you?'

Jabra barked as if to say, 'How could I feel cold now?'

'We should have thought of this plan before, then we'd never have become so chilled.' Jabra wagged his tail. 'Fine, now what say we jump over the fire? Let's see how we manage it. But if you get scorched I've got no medicine for you.'

Jabra looked fearfully at the fire.

'We mustn't tell Munni tomorrow or there'll be a row.'

With that he jumped up and cleared the fire in one leap. He got his legs singed but he did not care. Jabra ran around the fire and came up to him. Halku said, 'Go on, no more of this. Jump over the fire!' He leaped again and came back to the other side.

The leaves were all burned up. Darkness covered the orchard again. Under the ashes a few embers smouldered and when a gust of wind flew over them they stirred up briefly, then flickered out again.

Halku wrapped himself up in his shawl again and sat by the warm ashes, humming a tune. The fire had warmed him through but as the cold began to spread he felt drowsy. Jabra gave a loud bark and ran towards the field. Halku realised that this meant a pack of wild animals had probably broken into the field. They might be *bluebuck*. He distinctly heard the noise of their moving about. Then it seemed to him they must be grazing; he began to hear the sound of nibbling. He thought, 'No, with Jabra around no animal can get into the field; he'd rip it to shreds. I must've been mistaken. Now there's no sound at all. I must have been mistaken.'

He shouted, 'Jabra! Jabra!' Jabra went on barking and did not come to him.

Then again there was the sound of munching and crunching in the field. He could not have been mistaken this time. It really hurt to think about getting up from where he was. It was so comfortable there that it seemed intolerable to go to the field in this cold and chase after animals. He did not stir. He shouted at the top of his lungs, 'Hillo! Hillo! Hillo!'

Jabra started barking again. There were animals eating in his field just when the crop was ready. What a fine crop it was! And those cursed animals were destroying it. With a firm resolve he got up and took a few steps. But suddenly a gust of wind pierced him with a sting like a scorpion's so that he went back and sat again by the extinguished fire and stirred up the ashes to warm his chilled body.

Jabra was barking his lungs out, the bluebuck were devastating his field and Halku went on sitting peacefully near the warm ashes. His drowsiness held him motionless as though with ropes. Wrapped in his shawl, he fell asleep on the warmed ground near the ashes.

When he woke in the morning, the sun was high and Munni was saying, 'Do you think you're going to sleep all day? You came out here and had a fine time while the whole field was being flattened!'

Halku got up and said, 'Then you've just come from the field?'

'Yes, the whole field's ruined. And you could sleep like that! Why did you bother to put up the shelter anyway?'

Halku sought an excuse. 'I nearly died and just managed to get through the night and you worry about your crop. I'd such a pain in my belly that I can't describe it.'

Then the two of them walked to the edge of their land. He looked: the whole field had been trampled and Jabra was stretched out underneath the shelter as though he were dead.

They continued to stare at the ruined field. Munni's face was shadowed with grief but Halku was content. She said, 'Now you'll have to hire yourself out to earn some money to pay off the rent and taxes.'

With a contented smile Halku said, 'But I won't have to sleep nights out here in the cold.'

Stench of Kerosene

AMRITA PRITAM   1965
Translated from Paniabi bv Khushwant Singh

In this tale, set in the northern state of Himachal Pradesh, romantic love encounters tragedy as the hard demands of traditional family life are obeyed.

Outside, a mare neighed. Guleri recognised the neighing and ran out of the house. The mare was from her parents' village. She put her head against its neck as if it were the door to her father's house.

Guleri's parents lived in Chamba. A few miles from her husband's village which was on high ground, the road curved and descended steeply downhill. From this point one could see Chamba lying a long way away at one's feet. Whenever Guleri was homesick she would take her husband Manek and go up to this point. She would see the homes of Chamba twinkling in the sunlight and would come back with her heart aglow with pride.

Once every year, after the harvest had been gathered in, Guleri was allowed to spend a few days with her parents. They sent a man to bring her back to Chamba. Two of her friends too, who were married to boys outside Chamba, came home at the same time of year. The girls looked forward to the annual meeting, when they spent many hours every day talking about their experiences, their joys and sorrows. They went about the streets together. Then there was the harvest festival. The girls would have new dresses made for the occasion. They would have their *dupattas* dyed, starched and sprinkled with mica, they would put on glass bangles and silver earrings.

Guleri always counted the days to the harvest. When autumn breezes cleared the skies of the monsoon clouds, she thought of little besides her home in Chamba. She went about her daily chores – fed the cattle, cooked food for her husband's parents and then sat back to work out how long it would be before someone would come for her from her parent's village.

And now, once again, it was time for her annual visit. She caressed the mare joyfully, greeted her father's servant, Natu, and made ready to leave next day.

Guleri did not have to put her excitement into words, the expression on her face was enough. Her husband, Manek, pulled at his *hookah* and closed his eyes. It seemed either as if he did not like the tobacco, or that he could not bear to face his wife.

'You will come to the fair at Chamba, won't you? Come, even if it is only for the day,' she pleaded.

Manek put aside his *chillum* but did not reply.

'Why don't you answer me?' asked Guleri in a little temper. 'Shall I tell you something?'

'I know what you are going to say: "I only go to my parents once in a year." Well you have never been stopped before.'

'Then why do you want to stop me this year?' she demanded.

'Just this time,' pleaded Manek.

'Your mother has not said anything. Why do you stand in my way?' Guleri was childishly stubborn.

'My mother . . .' Manek did not finish his sentence.

On the long-awaited morning, Guleri was ready long before dawn. She had no children and therefore no problem of either having to leave them with her husband's parents or taking them with her. Natu saddled the mare as she took leave of Manek's parents. They patted her head and blessed her.

'I will come with you a part of the way,' said Manek.

Guleri was happy as they set out. Under her dupatta she hid Manek's flute.

After the village of Khajiar, the road descended deeply to Chamba. There Guleri took out the flute from beneath the dupatta and gave it to Manek. She took Manek's hand in hers and said, 'Come now, play your flute.' But Manek, lost in thought, paid no need. 'Why don't you play your flute?' asked Guleri, coaxingly. Manek looked at her sadly. Then, putting the flute to his lips, he blew a strange anguished wail of sound.

'Guleri, do not go away,' he begged her. 'I ask you again, do not go this time.' He handed her back the flute, unable to continue.

'But why?' she asked. 'You come over on the day of the fair and we will return together. I promise you, I will not stay behind.'

Manek did not ask her again.

They stopped by the roadside. Natu took the mare a few paces ahead to leave the couple alone. It crossed Manek's mind that it was at this time of the year, seven years ago, that he and his friends had come on this very road to go to the harvest festival in Chamba. And it was at this fair that Manek had first seen Guleri and they had bartered their hearts to each other. Later, managing to meet alone, Manek remembered taking her hand and telling her, 'You are like unripe corn – full of milk.'

'Cattle go for unripe corn,' Guleri had replied, freeing her hand with a jerk. 'Human beings like it better roasted. If you want me, go and ask my father for my hand.'

Amongst Manek's kinsmen it was customary to settle the *bride-price* before the wedding. Manek was nervous because he did not know the price Guleri's father would demand from him. But her father was prosperous and he had lived in cities. He had sworn that he would not take money for his daughter, but give her to a worthy young man of good family. Manek, he had decided, answered these requirements and, very soon after, Guleri and Manek were married. Deep in memories, Manek was roused by Guleri's hand on his shoulder.

'What are you dreaming of?' she teased him.

He did not answer. The mare neighed impatiently and Guleri, thinking of the journey ahead of her, rose to leave. 'Do you know the bluebell wood a couple of miles from here?' she asked. 'It is said that any one who goes through it becomes deaf.'

'Yes.'

'It seems to me as if you had passed through the bluebell wood. You do not hear anything that I say.'

'You are right, Guleri. I cannot hear anything that you are saying to me,' replied Manek with a deep sigh.

Both of them looked at each other. Neither understood the other's thoughts.

'I will go now. You had better return home. You have come a long way,' said Guleri gently.

'You have walked all this distance. Better get on the mare,' replied Manek.

'Here, take your flute.'

'You take it with you.'

'Will you come and play it on the day of the fair?' asked Guleri with a smile. The sun shone in her eyes. Manek turned his face away. Guleri, perplexed, shrugged her shoulders and took the road to Chamba. Manek returned to his home.

Entering the house, he slumped listlessly on his *charpoy*.

'You have been away for a long time,' exclaimed his mother. 'Did you go all the way to Chamba?'

'Not all the way; only to the top of the hill.' Manek's voice was heavy.

'Why do you croak like an old woman?' asked his mother severely. 'Be a man.'

Manek wanted to retort, 'You are a woman; why don't you cry like one for a change!' But he remained silent.

Manek and Guleri had been married seven years, but she had never borne a child and Manek's mother had made a secret resolve: 'I will not let it go beyond the eighth year.'

This year, true to her decision, she had paid five hundred rupees to get him a second wife and now she had waited, as Manek knew, for the time when Guleri went to her parents to bring the new bride home.

Obedient to his mother and to custom, Manek's body responded to the new woman. But his heart was dead within him.

In the early hours of one morning he was smoking his chillum when an old friend happened to pass by.

'Ho! Bhavani, where are you going so early in the morning?'

Bhavani stopped. He had a small bundle on his shoulder. 'Nowhere in particular,' he replied evasively.

'You must be on your way to some place or the other,' exclaimed Manek. 'How about a smoke?'

Bhavani sat down on his haunches and took the chillum from Manek's hands. 'I am going to Chamba for the fair,' he replied at last.

Bhavani's words pierced through Manek's heart like a needle. 'Is the fair today?'

'It is the same day every year,' replied Bhavani dryly. 'Don't you remember, we were in the same party seven years ago?' Bhavani did not say anything more but Manek was conscious of the other man's rebuke and he felt uneasy. Bhavani put down the chillum and picked up his bundle. His flute was sticking out of the bundle. Bhavani bade farewell to Manek and walked away. Manek's eyes remained on the flute till Bhavani disappeared from view.

Next afternoon, when Manek was in his fields, he saw Bhavani coming back but deliberately looked the other way. He did not want to talk to Bhavani or hear anything about the fair. But Bhavani came round the other side and sat down in front of Manek. His face was sad, lightless like a cinder.

'Guleri is dead,' he said in a flat voice.

'What?'

'When she heard of your second marriage, she soaked her clothes in kerosene and set fire to them.'

Manek, mute with pain, could only stare and feel his own life burning out.

The days went by. Manek resumed his work in the fields and ate his meals when they were given him. But he was like a man dead, his face quite blank, his eyes empty.

'I am not his spouse,' complained his second wife. 'I am just someone he happened to marry.'

But quite soon she was pregnant and Manek's mother was well pleased with her daughter-in-law. She told Manek about his wife's condition, but he looked as if he had not understood, and his eyes were still empty.

His mother encouraged her daughter-in-law to bear with her husband's moods for a few days. As soon as the child was born and was placed in his father's lap, she said, Manek would change.

A son was duly born to Manek's wife, and his mother, rejoicing, bathed the boy, dressed him in fine clothes and put him in Manek's lap. Manek stared at the babe in his lap. He stared a long time uncomprehending, his face as usual, expressionless. Then suddenly the blank eyes filled with horror, and Manek began to scream.

'Take him away!' he shrieked hysterically. 'Take him away! He stinks of kerosene.'

We Have Arrived in Amritsar

BHISHAM SAHNI 1976

Translated from Hindi by Bhisham Sahni

> The partition of the Indian subcontinent into Pakistan and India
> (Bangladesh split off later) was a time of great turbulence, when
> millions sought safety and a new life with people of their own religion.
> In this tale the Hindu narrator is travelling by train to the capital of the
> newly independent India, for the Independence Day celebrations. It is
> 1947. The train travels from the North-West Frontier of the subconti-
> nent, across the newly-created Muslim state of Pakistan, entering India
> at Harbanspura. It is when the train is actually crossing the border,
> from Jhelum on the Pakistani side to Amritsar, holy city of the Sikhs,
> on the Indian side, that feelings inside the compartment reflect the
> riots outside. The Sikh shows solidarity with the Hindus; the Muslim
> Pathans move to sit together. Yet the horrors cannot be averted.

There were not many passengers in the compartment. The Sardarji, sitting
opposite me, had been telling me about his experiences in the war. He had
fought on the Burmese front, and every time he spoke about the British
soldiers, he had a hearty laugh at their expense. There were three *Pathan*
traders too, and one of them, wearing a green *salwar kameez*, lay stretched on
one of the upper berths. He was a talkative kind of a person and had kept up a
stream of jokes with a frail-looking *babu* who was sitting next to me. The
babu, it seemed, came from Peshawar because off and on they would begin to
converse with each other in *Pushto*. In a corner, under the Pathan's berth, sat
an old woman telling beads on her rosary, with her head and shoulders
covered by a shawl. These were the only passengers that I can recollect being
in the compartment. There might have been others too, but I can't remember
them now.

The train moved slowly and the passengers chatted away. Outside the
breeze made gentle ripples across the ripening wheat. I was happy because I
was on my way to Delhi to see the Independence Day celebrations.

Thinking about those days it seems to me that we had lived in a kind of
mist. It may be that as time goes by all the activities of the past begin to float in

a mist, which seems to grow thicker and thicker as we move away further into the future.

The decision about the creation of Pakistan had just been announced and people were indulging in all kinds of surmises about the pattern of life that would emerge. But no one's imagination could go very far. The Sardarji sitting in front of me repeatedly asked me whether I thought *Mr Jinnah* would continue to live in Bombay after the creation of Pakistan or whether he would resettle in Pakistan. Each time my answer would be the same, 'Why should he leave Bombay? I think he'll continue to live in Bombay and keep visiting Pakistan.' Similar guesses were being made about the towns of Lahore and Gurdaspur too, and no one knew which town would fall to the share of India and which to Pakistan. People gossiped and laughed in much the same way as before. Some were abandoning their homes for good, while others made fun of them. No one knew which step would prove to be the right one. Some people deplored the creation of Pakistan, others rejoiced over the achievement of Independence. Some places were being torn apart by riots, others were busy preparing to celebrate Independence. Somehow we all thought that the troubles would cease automatically with the achievement of freedom. In that hazy mist there came the sweet taste of freedom and yet the darkness of uncertainty seemed continuously to be with us. Only occasionally through this darkness did one catch glimpses of what the future meant for us.

We had left behind the city of Jhelum when the Pathan sitting on the upper berth untied a small bundle, took out chunks of boiled meat and some bread, and began distributing it among his companions. In his usual jovial manner he offered some of it to the babu next to me.

'Eat it, babu, eat it. It will give you strength. You will become like us. Your wife too will be happy with you. You are weak because you eat *dal* all the time. Eat it, *dalkhor*.'

There was laughter in the compartment. The babu said something in Pushto but kept smiling and shaking his head.

The other Pathan taunted him further.

'O *zalim*, if you don't want to take it from our hands, pick it up yourself with your own hand. I swear to God that it is only goat's meat and not of any other animal.'

The third Pathan joined in: 'O son of a swine, who is looking at you here? We won't tell your wife about it. You share our meat and we shall share your dal with you.'

There was a burst of laughter. But the emaciated clerk continued to smile and shake his head.

'Does it look nice that we should eat and you should merely look on?' The Pathans were in good humour.

The fat *Sardarji* joined in and said, 'He doesn't accept it because you haven't washed your hands,' and burst out laughing at his own joke. He was reclining on the seat with half his belly hanging over it. 'You just woke up and immediately started to eat. That's the reason *babuji* won't accept food from your hands. There isn't any other reason.' As he said this he gave me a wink and guffawed again.

'If you don't want to eat meat, you should go and sit in a ladies' compartment. What business have you to be here?'

Again the whole compartment had a good laugh. All the passengers had been together since the beginning of the journey, a kind of informality had developed amongst them.

'Come and sit with me. Come, rascal, we shall sit and chat about *kissakhani.*'

The train stopped at a wayside station and new passengers barged into the compartment. Many of them forced their way in.

'What is this place?' someone asked.

'Looks like Wazirabad to me,' I replied, peering out of the window.

The train only stopped for a short time, but during the stop a minor incident occurred. A man got down from a neighbouring compartment and went to the tap on the platform for water. He had hardly filled his glass with water when suddenly he turned round and started running back towards his compartment. As he ran the water spilt out of the glass. The whole manner of his dash was revealing to me. I had seen people running like this before and knew immediately what it meant. Two or three other passengers, who were queuing at the tap also began running towards their compartments. Within a matter of seconds the whole platform was deserted. Inside our compartment, however, people were still chatting and laughing as before.

Beside me the babu muttered: 'Something bad is happening.'

Something really had happened but none of us could figure it out. I had seen quite a number of communal riots and had learnt to detect the slightest change in the atmosphere; people running, doors shutting, men and women standing on housetops, an uncanny silence all round – these were signs of riots.

Suddenly the sound of a scuffle was heard from the back-entrance to the compartment. Some passenger was trying to get into the compartment.

'No, you can't come in here,' someone shouted. 'There is no place here. Can't you see? No, no. Go away.'

'Shut the door,' someone else remarked. 'People just walk in as though it was their uncle's residence.'

Several voices were heard, speaking simultaneously.

As long as a passenger is outside a compartment and is trying desperately to get in, he faces strong opposition from those inside. But once he succeeds in entering, the opposition subsides and he is soon accepted as a fellow traveller, so much so that at the next stop, he too begins to shout at the new passengers trying to get in.

The commotion increased. A man in soiled, dirty clothes and with drooping moustache forced his way into the compartment. From his dirty clothes he appeared to be a sweet-vendor. He paid no attention to the shouts of protest of the passengers. He squeezed himself inside and turned around to try and haul in his enormous black trunk.

'Come in, come in, you too climb,' he shouted, addressing someone behind him. A frail, thin woman entered the door followed by a young dark girl of sixteen or seventeen. People were still shouting at them. The Sardarji had got up on his haunches.

Everyone seemed to be shouting at the same time: 'Shut the door. Why don't you?' 'People just come barging in.' 'Don't let anyone in.' 'What are you doing?' 'Just push him out, somebody . . .'

The man continued hauling in his trunk, while his wife and daughter shrank back and stood against the door of the toilet, looking anxious and frightened.

'Can't you go to some other compartment? You have brought womenfolk with you too. Can't you see this is a men's compartment?'

The man was breathless and his clothes were drenched with perspiration. Having pulled in the trunk, he was now busy collecting the other sundry items of his baggage.

'I am a ticketholder. I am not travelling without tickets. There was no choice. A riot has broken out in the city. It was an awful job, reaching the railway station . . .'

All the passengers fell silent except the Pathan who was sitting on the upper berth. He leaned forward and shouted, 'Get out of here! Can't you see there is no room here?'

Suddenly he swung out his leg and kicked the man. Instead of hitting the man, his foot landed squarely on the wife's chest. She screamed with pain, and collapsed on the floor.

There was no time for argument. The sweet-vendor continued to assemble his baggage into the compartment. Everybody was struck silent. After pulling in the heavy bundle he was struggling with the bars of a dismantled *charpoy*. The Pathan lost all patience.

'Turn him out, who is he anyway?' he shouted.

One of the other Pathans sitting on the lower berth got up and pushed the man's trunk out of the compartment.

In that silence only the old woman could be heard. Sitting in the corner, she muttered abstractedly, 'Good folk, let them come in. Come, child, come and sit with me. We shall manage to pass the time somehow. Listen to me. Don't be so cruel . . .'

The train began to move.

'Oh, the luggage! What shall I do about my luggage!' the man shouted, bewildered and nervous.

'*Pitaji*, half our luggage is still outside! What shall we do?' the girl cried out, trembling.

'Get down. Let's get down. There is no time,' the man shouted nervously, and throwing the big bundle out of the door, he caught hold of the door-handle, and hurried down. He was followed by his trembling daughter and his wife who still clutched at her chest and moaned with pain.

'You are bad people!' the old woman shouted. 'You have done a very bad thing. All human feeling has died in your hearts. He had his young daughter with him. There is no pity in your hearts . . .'

The train left the deserted platform and steamed ahead. There was an uneasy silence in the compartment. Even the old woman had stopped muttering. No one had the courage to defy the Pathans.

Just then the babu sitting next to me touched my arm and whispered agitatedly, 'Fire! Look! There is a fire out there!'

By now the platform had been left far behind and all we could see was clouds of smoke rising from the leaping flames.

'A riot has started! That's why the people were running about on the platform. Somewhere a riot has broken out!'

The whole city was aflame. When the passengers realised what was happening, they all rushed to the windows to get a better view of the inferno.

There was an oppressive silence in the compartment. I withdrew my head from the window and looked about. The feeble-looking babu had turned deathly pale, the sweat on his forehead was making it glisten in the light. The passengers were looking at each other nervously. A new tension could now be felt between them. Perhaps a similar tension had arisen in each compartment of the train. The Sardarji got up from his seat and came over and sat down next to me. The two Pathans sitting on the lower berth climbed up to the upper berth where their compatriot was sitting. Perhaps the same process was on in other compartments also. All dialogue ceased. The three Pathans, perched side by side on the upper berth, looked quietly down. The eyes of each passenger were wide with apprehension.

'Which railway station was that?' asked someone.

'That was Wazirabad.'

The answer was followed by another reaction. The Pathans looked perceptibly relieved. But the Hindu and Sikh passengers grew more tense. One of the Pathans took a small snuffbox out of his waistcoat and sniffed it. The other Pathans followed suit. The old woman went on with her beads but now and then a hoarse whisper could be heard coming from her direction.

A deserted railway platform faced us when the train stopped at the next station. Not even a bird anywhere. A water-carrier, his water-bag on his back, came over to the train. He crossed the platform and began serving the passengers with water.

'Many people killed. Massacre, massacre,' he said. It seemed as though in the midst of all that carnage he alone had come out to perform a good deed.

As the train moved out again people suddenly began pulling down the shutters over the windows of the carriage. Mingled with the rattle of wheels, the clatter of closing shutters must have been heard over a long distance.

The babu suddenly got up from his seat and lay down on the floor. His face was still deathly pale. One of the Pathans perched above the others said mockingly: 'What a thing to do! Are you a man or a woman? You are a disgrace to the very name of man!' The others laughed and said something in Pushto. The babu kept silent. All the other passengers too were silent. The air was heavy with fear.

'We won't let such an effeminate fellow sit in our compartment,' the Pathan said. 'Hey babu, why don't you get down at the next station and squeeze into a ladies' compartment?'

The babu stammered something in reply, and fell silent. But after a little while he quietly got up from the floor, and dusting his clothes went and sat down on his seat. His whole action was completely puzzling. Perhaps he was afraid that there might soon be stones pelting the train or firing. Perhaps that was the reason why the shutters had been pulled down in all the compartments.

Nothing could be said with any sense of certainty. It may be that some passengers, for some reason or the other, had pulled down a shutter and that others had followed suit without thinking.

The journey continued in an atmosphere of uncertainty. Night fell. The passengers sat silent and nervous. Now and then the speed of the train would suddenly slacken, and the passengers would look at one another with wide-open eyes. Sometimes it would come to a halt, and the silence in the compartment would deepen. Only the Pathans sat as before, unruffled and relaxed. They too, however, had stopped chatting because there was no one to take part in their conversation.

Gradually the Pathans began to doze off while the other passengers sat staring into space. The old woman, her head and face covered in the folds of her shawl, her legs pulled up on the seat, dozed off too. On the upper berth, one of the Pathans awoke, took a rosary out of his pocket and started counting the beads.

Outside, the light of the moon gave the countryside an eerie look of mystery. Sometimes one could see the glow of fire on the horizon. A city burning. Then the train would increase its speed and clatter through expanses of silent country, or slow down to an exhausted pace.

Suddenly the feeble-looking babu peeped out of the window and shouted, 'We have passed *Harbanspura*!' There was intense agitation in his voice. The passengers were all taken aback by this outburst and turned round to stare at him.

'Eh, babu, why are you shouting?' the Pathan with the rosary said, surprised. 'Do you want to get down here? Shall I *pull the chain*?' He laughed jeeringly. It was obvious that he knew nothing about the significance of Harbanspura. The location and the name of the town conveyed nothing to the Pathan.

The babu made no attempt to explain anything. He just continued to shake his head as he looked out of the window.

Silence descended on the passengers of the compartment once again. The engine sounded its whistle and slowed its pace immediately. A little later, a loud clicking sound was heard; perhaps the train had changed tracks. The babu peeping out of the window looked towards the direction in which the train was advancing.

'We are nearing some town,' he shouted. 'It is Amritsar.' He yelled at the top of his voice and suddenly stood up and, addressing the Pathan sitting on the upper berth, shouted, 'You son of a bitch, come down!'

The babu started yelling and swearing at the Pathan, using the foulest language. The Pathan turned round and asked, 'What is it, babu? Did you say something to me?'

Seeing the babu in such an agitated state of mind, the other passengers too pricked up their ears.

'Come down, *haramzade*. You dared kick a Hindu woman, you son of a . . .'

'Hey, control your tongue, babu! You swine, don't swear or I'll pull out your tongue!'

'You dare call me a swine!' the babu shouted and jumped on to his seat. He was trembling from head to foot.

'No, no, no quarrelling here,' the Sardarji intervened, trying to pacify them. 'This is not the place to fight. There isn't much of the journey left. Let it pass quietly.'

'I'll break your head,' the babu shouted, shaking his fist at the Pathan. 'Does the train belong to your father?'

'I didn't say anything. Everyone was pushing them out. I also did the same. This fellow here is abusing me. I shall pull out his tongue.'

The old woman again spoke beseechingly, 'Sit quietly, good folk. Have some sense. Think of what you are doing.'

Her lips were fluttering like those of a spectre, and only indistinct, hoarse whispers could be heard from her mouth.

The babu was still shouting, 'You son of a bitch, did you think you would get away with it?'

The train steamed into Amritsar railway station. The platform was crowded with people. As soon as the train stopped they rushed towards the compartments.

'How are things there? Where did the riot take place?' they asked anxiously.

This was the only topic they talked about. Everyone wanted to know where the riot had taken place. There were two or three hawkers, selling *puris* on the platform. The passengers crowded round them. Everyone had suddenly realised that they were very hungry and thirsty. Meanwhile two Pathans appeared outside our compartment and called out for their companions. A conversation in Pushto followed. I turned round to look at the babu, but he was nowhere to be seen. Where had he gone? What was he up to? The Pathans rolled up their beddings and left the compartment. Presumably they were going to sit in some other compartment. The division among the passengers that had earlier taken place inside the compartments was, now taking place at the level of the entire train.

The passengers who had crowded round the hawkers began to disperse to return to their respective compartments. Just then my eyes fell on the babu. He was threading his way through the crowd towards the compartment. His face was still very pale and on his forehead a tuft of hair was hanging loose. As he came near I noticed that he was carrying an iron rod in one of his hands. Where had he got that from? As he entered the compartment he furtively hid the rod behind his back, and as he sat down, he quickly pushed it under the seat. He then looked up towards the upper berth and not finding the Pathans there grew agitated and began looking around.

'They have run away, the bastards! Sons of bitches!'

He got up angrily and began shouting at the passengers: 'Why did you let them go? You are all cowards! Impotent people!' But the compartment was crowded with passengers and no one paid any attention to him.

The train lurched forward. The old passengers of the compartment had stuffed themselves with puris and had drunk enormous quantities of water; they looked contented because the train was now passing through an area where there was no danger to their life and property. The new entrants into the compartment were chatting noisily. Gradually the train settled down to an even pace and people began to doze. The babu, wide awake, kept staring into space. Once or twice he asked me about the direction in which the Pathans had gone. He was still beside himself with anger.

In the rhythmical jolting of the train I too was overpowered by sleep. There wasn't enough room in the compartment to lie down. In the reclining posture in which I sat my head would fall, now to one side, now to the other. Sometimes I would wake up with a start and hear the loud snoring of the Sardarji who had gone back to his old seat and had stretched himself full length on it. All the passengers were lying or reclining in such grotesque postures that one had the impression that the compartment was full of corpses. The babu however sat erect, and now and then I found him peeping out of the window.

Every time the train stopped at a wayside station, the noise from the wheels would suddenly cease and a sort of desolate silence descend over everything. Sometimes a sound would be heard as of something falling on the platform or of a passenger getting down from a compartment, and I would sit up with a start.

Once when my sleep was broken, I vaguely noticed that the train was moving at a very slow pace. I peeped out of the window. Far away, to the rear of the train, the red lights of a railway signal were visible. Apparently the train had left some railway station but had not yet picked up speed.

Some stray, indistinct sounds fell on my ears. At some distance I noticed a dark shape. My sleep-laden eyes rested on it for some time but I made no effort to make out what it was. Inside the compartment it was dark, the light had been put out some time during the night. Outside the day seemed to be breaking.

I heard another sound, as of someone scraping the door of the compartment. I turned round. The door was closed. The sound was repeated. This time it was more distinct. Someone was knocking at the door with a stick. I looked out of the window. There was a man there; he had climbed up the two steps and was standing on the footboard and knocking away at the door with a stick. He wore drab, colourless clothes, and had a bundle hanging from his shoulder. I also noticed his thick, black beard and the turban on his head. At some distance, a woman was running alongside the train. She was barefooted and had two bundles hanging from her shoulders. Due to the heavy load she was carrying, she was not able to run fast. The man on the footboard was again and again turning towards her and saying in a breathless voice: 'Come on, come up, you too come up here!'

Once again there was the sound of knocking on the door.

'Open the door, please. For the sake of Allah, open the door.'

The man was breathless.

'There is a woman with me. Open the door or we shall miss the train . . .'

Suddenly I saw the babu get up from his seat and rush to the door.

'Who is it? What do you want? There is no room here. Go away.'

The man outside again spoke imploringly: 'For the sake of Allah, open the door, or we shall miss the train.'

And putting his hand through the open window, he began fumbling for the latch.

'There's no room here. Can't you hear? Get down, I am telling you,' the babu shouted, and the next instant flung open the door.

'Ya Allah!' the man exclaimed, heaving a deep sigh of relief.

At that very instant I saw the iron rod flash in the babu's hand. He gave a stunning blow to the man's head. I was aghast at seeing this; my legs trembled. It appeared to me as though the blow with the iron rod had no effect on the man, for both his hands were still clutching the door-handle. The bundle hanging from his shoulder had, however, slipped down to his elbow.

Then suddenly two or three tiny streams of blood burst forth and flowed down his face from under his turban. In the faint light of the dawn I noticed his open mouth and his glistening teeth. His eyes looked at the babu, half-open eyes which were slowly closing, as though they were trying to make out who his assailant was and for what offence had he taken such a revenge. Meanwhile the darkness had lifted further. The man's lips fluttered once again and between them his teeth glistened. He seemed to have smiled. But in reality his lips had only curled in terror.

The woman running along the railway track was grumbling and cursing. She did not know what had happened. She was still under the impression that the weight of the bundle was preventing her husband from getting into the compartment, from standing firmly on the footboard. Running alongside the train, despite her own two bundles, she tried to help her husband by stretching her hand to press his foot to the board.

Then, abruptly, the man's grip loosened on the door-handle and he fell headlong to the ground, like a slashed tree. No sooner had he fallen than the woman stopped running, as though their journey had come to an end.

The babu stood like a statue, near the open door of the compartment. He still held the iron rod in his hand. It looked as though he wanted to throw it away but did not have the strength to do so. He was not able to lift his hand, as it were. I was breathing hard; I was afraid and I continued staring at him from the dark corner near the window where I sat.

Then he stirred. Under some inexplicable impulse he took a short step forward and looked towards the rear of the train. The train had gathered speed. Far away, by the side of the railway track, a dark heap lay huddled on the ground.

The babu's body came into motion. With one jerk of the hand he flung out the rod, turned round and surveyed the compartment. All the passengers were sleeping. His eyes did not fall on me.

For a little while he stood in the doorway undecided. Then he shut the door. He looked intently at his clothes, examined his hands carefully to see if there was any blood on them, then smelled them. Walking on tiptoe he came and sat down on his seat next to me.

The day broke. Clear, bright light shone on all sides. No one had pulled the chain to stop the train. The man's body lay miles behind. Outside, the morning breeze made gentle ripples across the ripening wheat.

The Sardarji sat up scratching his belly. The babu, his hands behind his head, was gazing in front of him. Seeing the babu facing him, the Sardarji giggled and said, 'You are a man with guts, I must say. You don't look strong, but you have real courage. The Pathans got scared and ran away from here. Had they continued sitting here you would certainly have smashed the head of one of them . . .'

The babu smiled – a horrifying smile – and stared at the Sardarji's face for a long time.

A Day with My Father

SUNDARA RAMASWAMY   1987
Translated from Tamil by Lakshmi Holmström

Technology, no manner how basic, brings progress – and can embarrass those who cannot cope with it. Even the humble telephone can cause problems. This gently ironic tale is set in an unnamed town which could well be the author's Nagercoil in the south-eastern state of Tamil Nadu. The young boy is a product of these modern times and copes with change so easily; but he is also a true member of his society and continues to respect the elders who can never hope to be part of the rapidly changing world in which he will grow up.

Uncle Raju was only a cousin of my father's. But the two were closer to each other than real brothers would have been. When my father's family lost all its money, and my father himself was left with his young bride, utterly helpless and without any means of livelihood, it was Uncle Raju who gave him a helping hand. It seems he transferred an agency which he owned, and which was bringing him a good income, into my father's name. It was from that moment, my father claimed, that he had been able to make his way in the world, to earn a few pennies and to hold his head up as a man. In the depths of his heart, my father was always aware that he owed this debt of gratitude to Raju. My mother fully shared in that feeling. Whenever the two of them spoke of Uncle Raju, they would be quite overcome. Because my mother had told us so often about all this, my sister Ramani and I had begun to think of Uncle Raju as being almost godlike.

Uncle Raju usually came to visit us once a year. On the instant the letter came, telling us of his visit, the whole house would begin to alter. My uncle liked to sleep on a rope bed. So the business of taking it out into the backyard and pouring boiling water over it to rid it of bedbugs would begin. My mother would make his favourite pickles and set about preparing various dried and spiced vegetables. My father would buy a new set of hand fans, decorated with gold thread. It was our habit, Ramani's and mine, to station ourselves on either side of Uncle Raju when he took a nap after his midday meal, and to fan him while he slept. Ramani always assigned the foot of the bed to me. She said I didn't have the skill of fanning him without actually touching his face. So, whenever my mother called Ramani away, I'd lean over and fan Uncle's face assiduously. Uncle Raju would smile on those occasions, even though his eyes were shut, letting me know he was aware of my tactics. The faint red of the betel leaves he had been chewing would be visible, rather beautifully, in that smile. Uncle Raju used to say that it was only the *veshtis* made by a particular weaver called Vadasseri Tanumal which suited him exactly in height and width. So my father would place an order for several veshtis in fine, *hundred-count cotton*, bordered elegantly in black. My mother and Aunt Ananda would go and inspect the banana trees in the backyard, in order to decide exactly which of the leaves they were going to take down. Somehow, Uncle Raju's visits always coincided with the occasions when the cow had calved. 'Who can share in that special good fortune of his in always being here at such a lucky time?' my father would say, with considerable pride.

Uncle Raju's family was quite a large one. 'A dozen and a quarter,' he used to say. This was only a slight exaggeration. In truth he had fourteen children. And there were nearly thirty grandsons and granddaughters. They lived as a joint family; there was a single kitchen where all the cooking was done. My parents had no doubt at all that Uncle Raju's visit to us, taking him away from his usual noisy surroundings, must be a real rest for him. If he began to show signs of wanting to return home, my father would say, 'Of course you can go any time, but what's the hurry?' and press him to stay longer. They would talk about their childhood days, always ending with the words, 'Now, of course, times have got worse. Everything has fallen to rack and ruin.' Yet they always had more to say when they woke up the next morning. My father would go off to open his shop, sad that he had to earn a livelihood, and could not therefore spend more time with Uncle Raju.

Telephones were not in common use in those days. One morning, at dawn, a messenger came to our house from the telephone office. There was a call for my father, it seemed, from Cochin. Both my father and mother were devastated. It was in Cochin that Uncle Raju lived. I wanted to study my father's face. Out of the question to go and stand directly in front of him. He was like a roaring fire, with endless tongues of flame separating themselves and reaching up to the roof. I took to my usual ploy in such circumstances: I climbed up the bright green *margosa* tree which grew to one side of the house, right against the garden wall, and positioned myself there. When the wind blew aside the window curtains of the rooms on that side of the house, I could see through to the front *veranda* where my father sat on an easy chair, his face aflame. In this way, I was able to look at him from time to time, and analyse his expression. Of course, Ramani didn't have this problem. If she was minded to, she could go straight away to the veranda. She'd even go and stand right by his side. Sometimes he'd look about him to make certain nobody was around and then draw her to his side and gently stroke her forehead. I had often seen this from my perch in the margosa tree. Because Ramani, too, knew where I was she'd look in my direction with a certain expression on her face. She wanted me to see that Father was making much of her. She wanted me to envy her good fortune. I pulled some terrible faces in return. If there wasn't a good enough breeze lifting the window curtains, I'd have to pull ten or twelve faces before I could be certain she had seen me.

Anyway, I was watching my father's face intently. It looked quite red. Whenever he was really worried or troubled, he would press the fingers of his left hand down against his chin, pushing up the flesh of his cheeks. His gaze would become fixed on a single spot. Sometimes he would shut his eyes and sigh deeply. You could imagine that all his worry was converted into the breath that he blew away. But I had never before seen such agitation in his face. As if he was soundlessly suffering some terrible internal pain.

I came down from my tree and towards the front of the house. I climbed up the veranda and leaned against a pillar. He did not say a thing to me. I suddenly became certain that he wasn't going to fly into a temper with me. I might even go right up and stand next to him. Nothing was going to happen. 'Call your mother,' he said. He had hardly ever spoken so gently to me. I climbed down the steps again and wiped my feet against the cement floor of the courtyard. My father must surely think I was being very particular. How could I demonstrate to them that I could act sensibly unless they allowed me the space to do it? It wasn't just Ramani who was endowed with a set of brains. Mine could work perfectly well too. It was just that I was never given a chance. I ran indoors.

Mother came and stood by the window that gave on to the veranda, and cleared her throat. That was her special position. The clearing of her throat signified her arrival. After this, my father would ask her various questions while he gazed at the street, the shrubs and creepers, the coconut palms and the moving birds. And Mother would address her replies to the back of his head. When he asked her certain confusing or contradictory questions, she would always answer him very patiently, reserving her grimaces and gestures for our benefit.

My father shouted somewhat loudly. 'There's not a soul about. I have to go there and see to it myself.' Ramani and I moved quietly to my mother's side. Through the gap in the window curtain, I could see well enough to count the moles and spots on my father's shoulders. In a sort of way, his shouting was justified. He was never one to go out and about. It was always either Uncle Seenu or Uncle Nataraj who ran his errands for him or saw to any outside business concerning us. Aunt Ananda had been known to put out the kitchen fire and go on an errand for him, leaving the cooking half-done. Perfectly true that he had not taken himself to the Post Office, nor to the Electricity Office, nor to the general grocery store, nor even, regarding his children's affairs, to the school or the hospital. Hadn't even gone down to the stall selling *betel leaves*. 'Let's wait a little and see if anyone turns up,' said my mother. My father shouted rather more loudly, 'Has anyone ever turned up to help me in an emergency? I have to see to every single thing myself.' Even at such a time, my mother was overcome by a fit of giggles. When she covered her mouth with her hand, Ramani at once imitated her gesture. I held my mouth with both hands, making as if it was harder for me to control my laughter than it was for the other two. I didn't want Ramani to think I hadn't understood the joke. Otherwise she'd plague me about it. Ramani was always looking for an opportunity to catch me out.

For a third time, my mother asked, 'Where did they say the call was from?' She asked this, although she was perfectly well aware of the answer, to try and calm his agitation. Father didn't reply. His silence meant, 'I can't be expected to talk to people who have no brains.'

All of a sudden, like one who was possessed by a religious frenzy, he thrust his feet into his sandals and hastened down the front steps. My mother was taken aback. 'You go with him, boy,' she called out to me. I was extremely surprised by her asking me to accompany him, as she normally agreed with my father that I was worth no more than a couple of pennies. By this time, my father, who had got as far as the front gate, turned round and yelled, 'Why do you want to send him?' 'He'll carry your umbrella for you,' she said. Nobody could match my mother at thinking fast in an emergency. How did she know so well that he would only allow me to go along with him if I had a small, relatively trivial job to do? I ran to his room, took up his umbrella, and clutched it to my chest. Nobody else had been allowed to touch it until that moment.

My father had gone quite some distance. He was hurrying along as if he didn't wish me to catch up with him. Would I allow that? I flew like the wind. He hadn't quite reached the grounds of the senior school. I came to a stop in front of him, staggering a little in order to indicate that if I hadn't braked so hard I might well have fallen on top of him. As soon as he saw me he said, 'Why couldn't you have put on a proper shirt, you idiot?' He didn't say 'idiot' in his usual way, though. Somehow the word seemed to come out, steeped in affection. 'I'll go back and change,' I said, turning around and preparing to leap off. 'No, no. Never mind. After all, you are only a little fellow.' I began to feel very happy when he said that. I felt as if a blazing flame had suddenly changed into a piece of ice which touched me comfortingly. And it wasn't just my imagination. My father had actually taken my hand in his. Such happiness! It was actually like a kind of electric charge. I ran along by his side, determined not to lag behind in the slightest. I held the umbrella tightly in my hand.

The telephone office was just next to the senior school. Just beyond its entrance was a rather wide veranda. There was a long bench on the righthand side. To the left, there was the glass-fronted booth with the telephone. My father would have to go inside it to take his call. I looked about me, observing everything minutely, and anxious that later on my father should speak of me to my mother with pride. He now sat down on the bench looking exhausted. His face looked even more tired out than before. The sweat was pouring down his neck. I felt ashamed that I had lost the opportunity to give him the umbrella, opened against the sun. I felt I really deserved to be called 'idiot'. I would put that right, though. I wished I could speak some words of comfort to him. I tried to think of the things that my mother would say in times like this. I thought how fortunate it would be if the call from Cochin turned out not to be for my father, after all.

I peeped inside the telephone office. There was a young woman with her hair in two plaits, at the desk right in front. Mother had instructed me with great care whom I should address as 'maami' or aunt, and whom I should address as 'akka' or elder sister. According to her teaching, this young woman was more than 'akka' but less than 'maami'. She had a gadget over her ears such as pilots wear and she kept pulling out and changing the knobs from the holes in the board in front of her. I called out to her, 'Akka,' and told her my father's name. Without opening her mouth she gestured with her left hand that we should wait. I went and sat next to my father. The seconds went past, like hours.

Suddenly the young woman called out my father's name and said, 'Sir, you may speak now.' My father jumped up in a great panic, pulled open the glass door of the booth, seized the receiver and, putting it against his ear, shouted very loudly, 'It's me. It's me.' The young woman said, 'Oh sir, please don't shout. Wait a second, I'm just getting the line.'

Because I too had opened the door in order to thrust my head inside, everybody had heard my father shouting. I thought I could make out that some of the people on the veranda were smiling. A young man who was lounging against a pillar smoking a cigarette, said to his friend, 'Where's the sense in saying, "It's me, it's me,"'? Why can't he give his name?' I understood beautifully. '*Appa*, say your name,' I told him. My father immediately shouted seven or eight times, 'It's me, Sankaran.' Then he looked at me and said with great bitterness and disappointment, 'Balu, I can't hear a thing.' I was overjoyed that he could share his troubles with me. I asked, 'Shall I speak, Appa?' Such impertinence! But like a child he handed the receiver to me and said, 'You speak.' I said, 'Hallo, hallo.' It went through my mind that he hadn't used that word, and that I had said it straight away, just out of the blue. 'But Appa, I can hear very clearly. It's Seenu speaking.' He spurred me on. 'Speak to him, speak to him.' 'It seems Uncle died. Seenu seems to be crying.' Overcome, my father plucked the receiver out of my hands and yelled, 'Has Raju gone, then?' The young woman's voice came to us from the office, 'Your three minutes are up, Sir.'

When we came past the secondary school building, my father suddenly sat down in the veranda, worn out. He just couldn't walk any further. His eyes filled and brimmed over on to his cheeks. He took his glasses off, folded them away into his pocket and covered his face with his handkerchief. With one arm he pulled me close to him. I felt terribly sorry for him. I wanted to grow as huge as the *Hanuman* in the Sudindram temple so that I could sling him across my shoulder and take off into the air, landing on the terrace of our house. I pulled at his hand. He rose to his feet and began to walk, as if he was spellbound.

My father went along one side of the house to the well that stood in our backyard. He began to pour some water over himself. Almost without thinking he poured some water over me as well. I felt very awkward. Ramani had come to the back veranda, where she was watching us. Completely forgetful of himself, in a kind of trance, my father kept pouring water over himself, long past the time that he should have stopped.

In spite of all my mother's entreaties, he refused to eat, and went to lie down. 'What's the good of just filling one's belly from time to time,' he said. Contrary to his usual custom, he just spread a mat on the floor and lay down on that. I fanned him with a hand fan. Very gently. I could sense that Ramani was staring at me. I paid no attention to her. There would be no need for me to bother about her any more. If he was her father, well, he was my father too.

When he woke up, Mother didn't ask him, 'Will you eat now?' She just laid a place for him and began serving his meal. He came and sat down just as she was spooning out the rice. He didn't say a word. He ate his meal as usual, with relish. As soon as he had finished and had gone out into the front veranda, my mother came to stand by the window. 'The telephone office is just next to the secondary school, isn't it?' she asked. This actually meant, tell me everything from start to finish. My father heaved a great sigh and began. I slipped down from the veranda on to the front courtyard without his noticing me, walked round to the back of the house, came inside and sat at my mother's feet. I wanted to hear him telling her all about my adventures.

As he spoke, though, things took a different turn. Not only did he not mention my having spoken into the telephone, he made out that he had managed everything himself, by his own skill. As for me, I had already made it a point to tell Ramani and my mother all that I had done. I now gave my mother's leg a sharp pinch. She asked, 'Did Balu carry your umbrella for you?'

'Why did you need to send him? Can't I carry my own umbrella? What does he know, he's only a child after all. Has he ever seen a telephone? Has he ever been inside a government office? Poor fellow, he came running after me.'

That evening, when Uncle Seenu and Uncle Nataraj came to visit us, my father described to them in great detail how we had had news of Uncle Raju's death. 'Death must come to us all,' he said, 'inevitably. No point in being too distressed.' My standing there in the veranda seemed to annoy him acutely. He shouted in my direction, 'Go in, boy! Take your books out and do your lessons.' Same old Appa. Once again the same old shout.

I went through the back of the house and climbed up the margosa tree. Ramani came by. As usual, I held on to the branches above me and let one of my feet dangle well down, in her direction. She grasped hold of it and climbed up. Tidying her skirt about her, she said, 'If you let loose a whole bundle of lies, none of it will stick, you know.'

I yelled at her, 'I swear to you in the name of God Hanuman. I spoke into the telephone. Appa held on to me.'

'Better not mention Hanuman when you are bragging and boasting,' said Ramani, curling her lips contemptuously.

I kept quiet for a while. I was seething with fury inside.

'Ramani, that other uncle who visits us sometimes, is he older than Uncle Raju or younger?' I asked.

'Oh, much older,' said Ramani.

'You wait. When he dies, there will be another telephone call. I'll go with Appa again to receive it. You'd better come and see. Then you'll know for sure.'

'Idiot,' said Ramani, 'don't talk nonsense.'

Glossary

Abba (Urdu)	father
Allahho Akbar (Urdu)	God is great (Muslim slogan)
anna	in the old coinage system there were sixteen annas to the rupee
Appa (Tamil)	father
arti	part of the ceremony of worship, when the sacred flame is circled around the holy image
Ayyappa	a warrior god, particular to Kerala
babu	used in 'We Have Arrived in Amritsar' as a semi-sarcastic form of address, meaning Hindu gentleman
Babuji (Hindi)	father (-ji is a respectful and affectionate form of address, often added to titles and names). Babuji can also be used more generally, like 'Sir'
baghbakhri	child's game
bazookas	hand-held rocket launchers
bearer	waiter
betel leaves	aromatic leaves wrapped around spices and chewed as a delicacy
Bhagavati	Goddess in the state of Kerala
Bhai Saheb (Hindi)	eldest brother. Saheb is added to show special respect
bhaiya/bhai	literally 'brother'. Also a courteous form of address
bhajias	savoury snacks
bidi	cheap Indian cigarette
bluebuck	large short-horned Indian antelope (*nilgai* in Hindi)
bougainvillaea	a common flowering creeper with abundant pink and purple flowers
bride price	in some communities, the prospective bridegroom makes a settlement of money before the marriage can be agreed
brinjal	aubergine or egg plant

cardamom	aromatic seed-pods, often chewed at the end of a meal
chapati	flat bread, basic food of many north Indians
charpoy (Hindi)	portable bedstead, string base on a bamboo frame
chembu (Malayalam)	small brass vessel, serving as a dipper
chillum (Hindi)	small clay pipe for smoking tobacco
compound	gardens or land surrounding a building, usually with a boundary wall
coolies	labourers, usually paid by the day
cot	portable bedstead, string base on a bamboo frame, called *charpoy* in Hindi
croton	garden plant with variegated leaves
dal	lentils
dalkhor	lentil-eater, vegetarian (derogatory)
daruwala	dealer in liquor
deeparadhana (Sanskrit and Malayalam)	evening worship with the lighting of lamps
dhobi (Hindi)	washerman. In former days the dhobi would collect a family's laundry on particular days, wash and iron the clothes and return them clean and neatly folded
dhoti (Hindi)	length of material worn by men, wrapped around and tied at the waist
Dipper	the American name for the constellation The Plough
dupatta	scarf or stole, worn with the Panjabi dress salwar kameez (Hindi)
edakka	musical instrument, particular to Kerala temples
Flit	a brand of insecticide
gallery	in 'Can You Hear Silence?', a small exposed space at the back of the flat, rather like a broom cupboard, not to be confused with the corridor connecting the front doors, where the children play, nor with the balcony overlooking the street
Ganesha	elephant-headed god, son of Shiva and Parvati
Ganga	correct (i.e. Sanskrit) name of the river also known as Ganges
ghee	clarified butter, used as a cooking medium
gopuram (Malayalam from Sanskrit)	temple tower, typically south Indian
Guru	honoured teacher and instructor

Gymkhana Grounds	sports club grounds
Halku	the name is derived from Hindi *halka*, which means light in weight
Hanuman	monkey god who plays an important part in the epic poem *Ramayana*. He was able to fly, jumped from India to Sri Lanka in one bound, and performed many wonderful exploits
Har Har Mahadev (Hindi)	Hari, great God. (Hindu slogan)
haramzade	extremely offensive abusive name
Harbanspura	the name indicates that it is a Sikh town, and in India
henna	a rich red stain obtained by crushing the henna leaf, and used as a cosmetic
henna blossom	flower of the same shrub, whose leaves are crushed to extract a deep red stain
hibiscus	flowering shrub
hookah	water tobacco-pipe
hundred-count cotton	number of strands of cotton to the inch, indicating the fineness of the weave
Id	breaking of fast and celebration, immediately after the rigours of Ramadan. The festival begins as soon as the new moon is sighted
idlis	steamed rice cakes
image	statue of a god
jacana	graceful aquatic bird, able to walk on the floating leaves of aquatic plants
jamun	dark-skinned, sweet and sour fruit
ji	suffix added to titles and names as additional respect or formality
kissakhani	narration of a traditional prose romance. Used loosely in 'We Have Arrived in Amritsar' to mean gossip. These Pathans are from Peshawar, where there is a Kissakhani Street (Street of Story-tellers)
Krishna	human incarnation of God Vishnu, who appears in many myths and cycles of legend, and in the epic poem, *Mahabharata*
kumkum	vermilion powder
major-domo	head servant

margosa	tree with bright green leaves, prized for its medicinal properties
Masterji	respectful form of Siddique Master, used for the tailor in 'Birthday'
Mr Jinnah	leader of the Muslim League before Independence. First Prime Minister of Pakistan
Namboodiri	Brahmins (of the highest caste) of Kerala. In former times, the women always carried umbrellas which screened them from the public gaze
narial	tender-coconut water
Om	sacred syllable, often preceding chants and prayers
paan (Hindi)	aromatic betel leaf wrapped around spices for chewing
paddy	unhusked rice
paisa	in the new coinage system, there are 100 paise to the rupee. (The paisa is not to be confused with 'pice' – see 'January Night'.) For some time, both coinages were in circulation side by side
Panjabi	both a language and one who speaks it; also one who lives in the state of Panjab
pappadam	very crisp savouries, eaten along with rice and other dishes
parathas	a kind of layered and fried bread
Parvati	goddess, wife of the god Shiva, with whom she is worshipped
Pathans	people from the former North-West Frontier area, now in Pakistan
pice	small denomination belonging to the old coinage system, four to an anna
Pitaji (Hindi)	Father (quite a formal mode of address)
plantain leaf	food is often wrapped in and served on plantain (banana plant) leaves. The leaves are very long, broad, waterproof and easily disposable
pleader	lawyer
pulling the chain	in 'We Have Arrived in Amritsar', refers to the emergency chain in railway carriages, which brings the train to a stop when pulled
puri	small circles of fried and puffed-up bread

Pushto	the language of the Pathans
Ram	one of the names of the God Vishnu
Ramadan	ninth month of the Islamic year, rigorously observed by Muslims as a thirty-day fast during the hours of daylight
road engine	motorised engine, fitted with a heavy cylindrical roller. It was used to smooth road surfaces and level them out
rupee	Indian currency
Sala!	rude term of abuse (like 'bastard!')
salwar kameez	loose trousers and tunic. The version worn by women usually adds a stole (*dupatta*)
samosa	fried savoury pastry
sandal paste	sweet-smelling paste of sandalwood
Sardar	title often given to Sikhs
sigri	portable coal stove
Sikh	follower of the religion known as Sikhism, founded by Guru Nanak in the sixteenth century. Sikhs largely lived in the Panjab and suffered the brunt of Partition, when their state was divided between India and Pakistan
soda-man	vendor of bottled drinks
subedar (Hindi)	sergeant
Swamiji	holy man
sweet betel	see 'paan'
tailoring house	small establishment making clothes to order. Most Indians, women in particular, have their clothes made to measure. (See also 'Passage'.) Until recently, ready-to-wear clothes were more expensive than made-to-measure clothes, but that is now changing
tank	artificial pond or reservoir attached to older houses and to all temples where it is obligatory to have a bath before worship
thali	large metal plate, usually with a rim
tilak	spot of vermilion powder that is placed on the forehead
to touch someone's feet	mark of respect. In 'A Trip to the City' Rai and Dulal are not related, but treat each other as brothers. So Rai becomes an honorary brother-in-law to Giri

Urdu	one of India's languages, similar to Hindi. Specially but not exclusively associated with Muslims, like the tailor Masterji in 'Birthday'. (Tailors in India are often Muslims: see 'Passage'.)
veranda	open portico with pillars and roof, running along the front of a house, and often all round it
veshti	length of cotton or silk material, usually white with narrow borders, worn by men, wrapped around the waist and tied
vibhuti (Sanskrit)	sacred ash, distributed by the priest to worshippers
Vir Chakra (Sanskrit and Hindi)	literally 'hero's discus'. A decoration awarded for bravery in battle
yakshi	statue of female supernatural being
Yoga, yogic	system of ascetic practices, meditation, etc., by which certain powers are said to be gained
zalim	tyrant (used sarcastically in 'We Have Arrived in Amritsar')
zari	gold-thread work